BrightRED Study Guide

CfE ADVANCED Higher

ENGLISH

Dr Christopher Nicol and
Dr Sandra Percy

First published in 2018 by:
Bright Red Publishing Ltd
1 Torphichen Street
Edinburgh
EH3 8HX

Copyright © Bright Red Publishing Ltd 2018

Cover image © Caleb Rutherford

All rights reserved. No part of this publication may be reproduced, stored in a retrieval system, or transmitted in any form or by any means, electronic, mechanical, photocopying, recording or otherwise, without prior permission in writing from the publisher.

The rights of Dr Christopher Nicol and Dr Sandra Percy to be identified as the authors of this work have been asserted by them in accordance with Sections 77 and 78 of the Copyright, Designs and Patents Act 1988.

A CIP record for this book is available from the British Library.

ISBN 978-1-849483-06-3

With thanks to:
Sue Lyons (editorial) and PDQ Digital Media Solutions (layout)
Cover design and series book design by Caleb Rutherford – e i d e t i c.

Acknowledgements
Every effort has been made to seek all copyright-holders. If any have been overlooked, then Bright Red Publishing will be delighted to make the necessary arrangements.

Permission has been sought from all relevant copyright holders and Bright Red Publishing are grateful for the use of the following:

Extracts from Tennessee Williams A Streetcar Named Desire. Copyright © 1947 The University of the South, renewed 1975 (p 16); Extracts from Tennessee Williams Cat on a Hot Tin Roof. Copyright © 1954, 1955, renewed 1982, 1983 by The University of the South (p 17); Extracts from A McArthur & H Kingsley Long No Mean City, first published by Longmans, Green and Company 1935. Published by Corgi 1957, a division of The Random House Group Ltd. (pp 22–23); Extracts from William McIlvanney Laidlaw. Copyright © William McIlvanney, 1977. Published by Canongate Books Ltd. (pp 22–23); Extracts from Sylvia Plath, "Tulips"; and "Nick and the Candlestick" taken from Collected Poems. Copyright © The Estate of Sylvia Plath, 1960, 1965, 1971, 1981, 1989. Published by Faber and Faber Ltd (pp 24–25); Extract from Sylvia Plath, "The Moon and the Yew Tree" from Ariel. Copyright © The Estate of Sylvia Plath, 1965. Published by Faber and Faber Ltd (p 25); Photo of Marlon Brando in A Streetcar Named Desire, Library of Congress, Prints & Photographs Division, Carl Van Vechten Collection (p 35); Extract from Lauren Seigle "Blanche Dubois: An Antihero" on Tennessee Williams's A Streetcar Named Desire by, taken from http://www.bu.edu/writingprogram/journal/past-issues/issue-2/seigle/. Reproduced by permission of Lauren Seigle (p 35); Extract from Colm Tóibín Brooklyn. Copyright © Colm Tóibín, 2009. First published by Viking 2009. Published by Penguin 2015 (p 42); Extract from George Orwell 1984. Copyright © the Estate of the late Sonia Brownell Orwell. Published by Penguin 2004 (p 43); Paolo Uccello Saint George and the Dragon. Copyright © The National Gallery, London. Bought with a special grant and other contributions, 1959 (p 51); Extract from Tennessee Williams The Glass Menagerie. Copyright © 1945 The University of the South, renewed 1973 (p 52); Extract from John McGrath The Cheviot, the Stag, and the Black, Black Oil. Published by Methuen Drama, an imprint of Bloomsbury Publishing Ltd. Copyright © John McGrath (p 55); Poem by Alan Riach "The Blues". Reproduced by permission of Alan Riach, first published in This Folding Map (Auckland University Press, 1990) (p 67); Extract from Richard Sterling The Fire Never Dies, copyright © 2001, Travelers' Tales (p 71); Steven Pisano (CC BY 2.0)1 (p 72); Extracts from Ted Hughes "The Hawk in the Rain" from The Hawk in the Rain. Copyright © Ted Hughes, 1957. Published by Faber & Faber Ltd (pp 84–5); Extracts from Ted Hughes "Hawk Roosting" from Lupercal. Copyright © The Estate of Ted Hughes, 1960, 1998. Published by Faber & Faber Ltd (pp 84–5).

(CC BY 2.0) https://creativecommons.org/licenses/by/2.0/

Printed and bound in the UK by Ashford Colour Ltd

CONTENTS

INTRODUCTION
Welcome to Advanced Higher English 4
Criteria for success 6
Key features for success............................. 8

DISSERTATION
What are you being asked to do? 10
Finding a topic..................................... 12
Taking notes (part 1) 14
Taking notes (part 2) 16
Thinking of topics and titles 18
Planning.. 20
Structuring 22
Structuring and linkage 24
Introductions – case studies (part 1)............... 26
Introductions – case studies (part 2)............... 28
Conclusions (part 1)................................ 30
Conclusions (part 2)................................ 32
The craft of writing (part 1)....................... 34
The craft of writing (part 2)....................... 36
Creating a bibliography 38

PORTFOLIO
Approaching portfolio writing 40
Prose fiction (part 1) 42
Prose fiction (part 2) 44
Reflective.. 46
Persuasive 48
Poetry 50
Drama... 52
Practicalities of drama 54
Argumentative....................................... 56

TEXTUAL ANALYSIS
What are you being asked to do? 58
Commenting on poetry 60
Formal structures and their usefulness.............. 62
Formal structures: rhythm and rhyme................. 64
Free verse and cohesion............................. 66
Commenting on prose fiction......................... 68
Non-fiction prose 70
Commenting on drama................................. 72

LITERARY STUDY
What are you being asked to do? 74
Developing ideas and opinions 76
Dissecting the questions 78
Constructing the essay.............................. 80
Structuring essays on more than one text............ 82

Writing about more than one poem.................... 84
Writing about more than one novel................... 86
Writing about more than one play 88
Top tips for revision............................... 90

FINAL EDITING PROCESS
Dissertation and portfolio 92
Detailed checks..................................... 94

INDEX 96

INTRODUCTION

WELCOME TO ADVANCED HIGHER ENGLISH

MOVING UP

These last few years, you and your English studies have come a long way. Now, Advanced Higher English will take all the hard-won skills you have acquired in understanding, analysing and evaluating complex texts to the next level. As you explore the structure, form and language of your selected texts in increasing depth, you will have the satisfaction of developing your critical capacities to respond to them with growing sophistication of expression.

Furthermore, you will have an opportunity to display your knowledge of structure, form and language creatively. For it offers you opportunities to produce a range of complex and sophisticated texts of your own, synthesising personal ideas and arguments.

These are communication skills which are vital for life in the twenty-first century and which, more specifically, can prepare you for:

- degree programmes in English, drama, education, humanities, journalism, law, media, business and social science
- careers in commerce and industry, education, journalism, law, marketing, media and politics.

FOLLOW THE GUIDE!

Advanced Higher English is a challenging course, but there is no need to feel daunted by it. This Study Guide, like the course itself, divides into four sections:

- Dissertation Production
- Portfolio Writing
- Textual Analysis
- Literary Study

Each section will indicate what the assessment will require of you, before suggesting practical methods of preparing for the various challenges in each area.

Useful, worked examples will highlight key points being made and ideal ways to answer questions.

Extra practice questions will help you improve on skills targeted at the end of each chapter.

To make the preparation process more approachable, we've built in handy 'Don't Forget' text boxes where key points are re-formed into nugget-sized reminders of essential facts and information. 'Things to do and think about' boxes are also featured regularly. These make helpful suggestions about various preparatory exercises and study areas you might productively consider.

So, let's get started!

Introduction: Welcome to Advanced Higher English

THE PROGRAMME AHEAD

There are four major challenges to be met in order to complete the Advanced Higher English programme.

Two of these challenges you will work on over the course of the year; two you will complete under examination conditions in the summer term. The course will be graded A–D. But let's break that down a little more.

Dissertation

Your dissertation counts for 30% of your overall mark and will be graded A–D. It should be between 2500 and 3000 words on an aspect of literature drawn from substantial texts agreed upon by you and your teacher.

As you might expect at Advanced Higher level, you are expected to demonstrate both knowledge of literary forms and genres and the ability to apply this to understanding complex and sophisticated literary texts. And once this is achieved, you need to be able to plan, research and present your findings from primary and secondary sources in dissertation form. Texts selected for dissertation purposes must be untaught. Like your portfolio, you will work on your dissertation over the course of the year.

Portfolio

Like your dissertation, the portfolio of writing accounts for 30% of your overall mark. It, too, will be graded A–D. The portfolio consists of two pieces in different genres worth a maximum of 15 marks each. Here, to do yourself full justice, you need to be conscious of the importance not just of content but also of structure, stance, tone, mood and accurate expression. Each piece should be at least 1000-words long, with the exception of poetry which may be shorter. You will work on these portfolio pieces over the course of the year.

Textual Analysis

Textual Analysis will be assessed in an examination of 90 minutes. The text for analysis will come from the genres of either poetry, prose fiction, prose non-fiction or drama. You should attempt only one question. Here, you are asked to offer a critical analysis of an unseen text. The good news is that you can write either a critical essay or respond to your selected text in extended bullet points. Textual Analysis accounts for 20% of your final grade.

Literary Study

Like Textual Analysis, Literary Study will be assessed in an examination of 90 minutes. In this, you will be offered a selection of questions from four genres: poetry, prose fiction, prose non-fiction or drama. You will answer only one question from your selected genre. You may not discuss text(s) from your dissertation. Answers should take the form of a critical essay, which will account for 20% of your final grade.

 **DON'T FORGET**

There may be moments when you find the course really challenging. But keep in mind that you have a proven record of success in this subject. A methodical approach to study; discussions with your teachers and peers; a willingness to draft and redraft; and a little assistance from us will go far to seeing you through!

 THINGS TO DO AND THINK ABOUT

It's never too early to start thinking about the subject of your dissertation. Yes, the start of the autumn term seems a long way from submission date, but time is shorter than you think. While the title itself may still be elusive, the general area of research and possible texts need to be considered now. Remember, you are expected to know these texts in depth; so, you need to get down to a reading programme as soon as you can.

INTRODUCTION

CRITERIA FOR SUCCESS

This course invites four different tasks which pose four distinct challenges. But once you start preparing for them, you'll notice that there's a common thread running through most of them. Or perhaps it would be more accurate to say that there are three threads: understanding, analysis and evaluation.

Now, you are familiar with these terms from earlier years, but before setting out on this demanding course, it might be a good idea to take one final look at these three terms to be certain you are totally familiar with the implications of all three for the Dissertation, Literary Study and Textual Analysis components. This will be time well spent, since your assessors will be scrutinising your work for clear evidence of all three.

UNDERSTANDING

This might appear to be the most straightforward of the three elements. But make sure you cover all bases.

What's happening here?

Of course, understanding entails being able to say what the text is about, at least what it is about on the surface. (A poem might – superficially – be about the meeting of two soldiers in the trenches, but, in your closer analysis, you might well discover that, at a deeper level, it's about the futility of war.) But the following aspects also need to be checked out to demonstrate a sound understanding.

Speaker identity

Check out the identity of the speaker or narrator. Is it the writer speaking as himself/herself? Is the writer speaking through a persona? A child, an old woman, a war veteran? In your later analysis, you will need to say how you worked this out and what the effect of this voice had on you.

Author's attitude

What appears to be the author's attitude to the people or topic they are writing about? Are they reflective, humorous, ironic, indignant? Again, in your later analysis, you'll need to say how the author indicated this.

Themes

What appears to be the wider theme lying behind these events which you have been describing? It will probably be too early to say definitively, of course, but are there any hints? How this theme (or themes) is realised will be your task in your later analysis.

ANALYSIS

Candidates sometimes get carried away with their command of literary/dramatic techniques and devices, hiding behind their sound knowledge of metaphors, onomatopoeia, sentence structure, symbols, etc. A sound knowledge of all these is important at this stage but, as we shall see in the following sections, being alert merely to their presence is not enough for success in Dissertation, Literary Study and Textual Analysis tasks.

Devices/techniques

What is of paramount importance is your ability to say how authors use devices and techniques to realise their intentions for their characters, settings or themes. (Repeated

contd

references to the symbol of fog, for instance, might suggest not only an effective setting but also the difficulty of seeing clearly in a world where the truth is easily obscured.) It is the effect on the reader/spectator that counts.

Word choice

Word choice is similarly helpful for deciding what authors' attitudes to the characters and settings created or the themes explored.

Tone

The author's use (or non-use) of literary devices and techniques, along with their word choices, will also help you determine the tone of the writer. Be aware that tone might alter over the course of the text. (If you need to remind yourself of some of the more common tone indicators, see Bright Red's Study Guide for CfE Higher English pp. 22–23.)

Mood

Be careful not to confuse tone with mood. Tone tells you about the writer's feelings towards their subject. Mood is what we readers are made to feel in our reaction to the created text. By this stage, you're probably quite able to track down tone indicators; but be careful not to overlook saying what your own mood is in reading the text. For instance, a writer may describe with biting humour a scene which fills you with anguish, anger or indignation.

When analysing a text, make sure you give full weight to the effect the writer's craft has on you; it's not enough simply to discuss its existence.

EVALUATION

Evaluation is probably the area of criticism which gives students most cause for reflection. Sometimes, candidates run away with the false idea that evaluation simply means saying whether you think a text is good or bad. (Although if examiners thought the text was unworthy of detailed study, why would they be offering it to you?!) No, your evaluation is to do with your personal response to the text and to the ideas which the author is putting forward. Your reaction may take various forms:

a) Do you agree or disagree with the attitude/views expressed? To what extent are you in agreement/disagreement with the author?

b) Can you see aspects of the text which have particular meaning or relevance to your life? Or to the social group to which you belong? Has the passing of time reduced/increased the text's relevance?

c) Has the writer's treatment of the topic altered your understanding of the issues at the heart of the text? Has it deepened your understanding?

d) Were there any aspects of the writer's craft which you found particularly successful in depicting character or illustrating themes? (Use of personification, symbolism, etc.)

DON'T FORGET

Critical analysis plays a major part in this course. It requires you to be totally familiar with literary terms and vocabulary. But do not hide behind critical language: ask yourself how these are helping what seem to be the writer's intentions; and keep in mind the need to adopt an evaluative stance of your own to this language. It's your response to it that the assessors want to know about.

 THINGS TO DO AND THINK ABOUT

Critical analysis, like life itself, can't always be separated into neat, closed-off compartments. Writing about literature – and importantly – assessing it, is seen as a holistic activity. Holistic? The OED defines it as being 'characterized by the belief that the parts of something are intimately interconnected'. Of course, your text requires an easy-to-follow structure of sequenced ideas which clearly set out your understanding, analysis and evaluation. You may find, however, that when analysing and evaluating, the line between the two becomes a little blurred. Your assessors are equally well aware of this. What is important is that your understanding, analysis and evaluation have plenty of solid evidence to support them.

INTRODUCTION
KEY FEATURES FOR SUCCESS

We've already emphasised the importance demonstrating skills in understanding, analysing and evaluating when responding to a range of complicated and sophisticated texts. But each of the four course components has its own particular demands.

In the following chapters, we take you step-by-step through these demands. But before we do, let's look at some of the key features of the course components.

DON'T FORGET

Being up to speed with the main elements required for successful Dissertation Production, Portfolio Writing, Textual Analysis and Literary Study will boost your confidence when you get down to tackling the detail of the course.

DISSERTATION

Overview

The dissertation, although possibly a new task for you, enables you to explore texts of your own choice and, as with other elements of the course, allows you to express your own interests and personality. Mastering its discipline will pay major dividends in any university or college career. Whatever genre or texts you choose to examine, you can make full use of your existing knowledge of genres and discuss text-specific points in satisfying detail. Always be flexible in your approach because your ideas may change as you read and explore in more depth.

Before you start

This is a moment for some intense reflection. Why have I chosen these particular texts? How well do I really know them? What will be the focus and title of my dissertation? Getting sound answers to these questions lies at the heart of dissertation success. It should be allotted plenty of thought. But there are other points to consider, too. How will I make notes to help me write it? How will I plan and structure it? Which quotations are most effective? How will I footnote and reference it? How will I manage my time?

Investing for the future

Writing a dissertation is useful preparation for writing assignments at university or college. While the regulations regarding word limits, the bibliography and submission dates must be respected, these – far from imposing a straight-jacket on your thoughts – provide a helpful discipline in marshalling your ideas in a timely and scholarly manner. Although dissertation writing may be new to you, the key to success here lies in refining and extending your skills from earlier English studies.

DON'T FORGET

Texts used in your dissertation must be untaught. And writers or texts studied for your dissertation cannot be used in the Literary Study exam … Good reason to start a full reading programme right now!

PORTFOLIO WRITING

The good news is your choice of genres is more open than it was in N5 or Higher. There's no obligation to write one discursive piece and one creative piece. As long as you write in two different genres, the choice is all yours: persuasive, argumentative, informative, reflective, poetry, prose fiction, or drama.

However, whichever genres you select, remember that they must present you and your capabilities at your very best. Choose carefully. In which genres do you feel most at ease? In which genres have you done well before?

Genre and genre markers

Each genre has a distinctive character. To succeed, you must get under the skin of your chosen genre. Read widely in that genre to absorb how professional writers set about a task similar to yours. Familiarise yourself with a broad range of writers and journalists to see how they develop plot, character and setting (in creative fiction) or arguments and ideas (in discursive writing).

contd

Introduction: Key features for success

Assessment criteria

The joy of the portfolio is that it allows you to explore your own personality and interests. While it is highly rewarding to create your own texts, you must also remember that these folio pieces will face the scrutiny of professional assessors. They'll look for thoughtful, rich content; a well-planned structure which does full justice to the content; tone and register appropriate to the task; and skilful use of style, technique and language. Offer your best on all four fronts!

TEXTUAL ANALYSIS

Overview

What's this text about? What's its effect on me? How has the writer created this effect? These questions should be at the front of your mind as you read.

Form and structure

Whether poetry, prose or drama, why has the writer shaped their material in this way? Is the poem written in regular lines and verse patterns? Or is it more loosely structured? In a prose text, how has the writer ordered their material? How does the paragraph sequence help us understand/follow their intentions? How do we react to the writer's choices?

Voice

Who's speaking? How does this voice shape the relationship with the audience? What tone is being adopted here? How do we react to this tone?

Word choice

In what kind of register is the text delivered? Is the vocabulary chatty and conversational? Or, are the words more formal or elaborate? Are the words rich in associated meanings or ambiguous possibilities?

Evocative imagery, rhythm and sound

In poetry, has the writer used imagery to guide our response to the subject? In poetry and prose, how has the actual sound of the words selected contributed to our reaction? In poetry, how has the rhythm or rhyme supported the writer's intentions? In prose, how has sentence structure affected our response?

These are just some of the questions you should ask yourself when approaching the texts in this course. See the chapter on textual analysis, where we help you work out answers to these questions.

LITERARY STUDY

Overview

This part of the exam combines the familiar and the new. You're no stranger to writing about literary texts, a task which remains central to this paper. However, now, you're expected to critically evaluate more than one text in your answer. You're required to compare and contrast the texts on which you have chosen to write. More emphasis is placed on your ability to adopt a personal stance – something which is good preparation for future study in all areas.

Making a start

As always, you begin by reading the question carefully and spending some time thinking. Which genre do I enjoy most? Which texts can I critically discuss and evaluate? Which texts do I hold an evaluative stance about? How do I structure my answer? Remember, you'll never be asked the 'perfect' question for what you have studied. Be prepared to be flexible.

Assessment criteria

As before, your professional assessors will be looking for knowledge and understanding of your chosen texts, but your discussions should explore this in greater depth. Now, your own personal stance and opinion are of prime importance. This, along with your analysis, will be an integral part of the structure that you adopt.

 ## THINGS TO DO AND THINK ABOUT

Advanced Higher English prepares you for college or university in many ways. Discussing various challenges with fellow students prepares you for tutorial work at the next stage of your education. Share your ideas about your dissertation and portfolio tasks. Articulating a problem to someone else can clarify your own thinking, and the views of others could help you see the flaws in your original ideas. Make discussion central to your preparation before and during the writing process.

DISSERTATION

WHAT ARE YOU BEING ASKED TO DO?

The SQA defines the dissertation as providing candidates with 'an opportunity to demonstrate the following skills: knowledge and understanding, independent planning, research and presentation of their knowledge, and understanding of an aspect or aspects of literature', and that 'The text(s) chosen must not be the same as those used in the Literary Study question paper. This dissertation will be between 2500 and 3000 words long and will be awarded 30 marks (30% of the total mark)'.

This can initially seem quite daunting and it's important that you understand what this means for you and the work you are about to embark on.

DON'T FORGET

All SQA coursework has a 10% tolerance and so the upper limit is 3300 words.

WHAT IS A DISSERTATION?

The difference between a dissertation and an essay

For the last five years, and probably even before that, you've been writing essays about the novels, poems and plays which you have read. In the case of the poems and plays, these will probably have been chosen by your teachers who will have set you a specific task or choice of tasks to write about. Frequently, the novels you'll have written about – particularly in the late primary and early secondary years – will have been of your own choice, but you will have probably been provided with a template or basic plan to follow.

In the case of a dissertation, you'll be choosing the subject for yourself, and you'll be required to plan it for yourself.

Content

As in previous years, you'll be required to show knowledge of your chosen texts but, this time, you won't have your teacher's help or notes to rely on. This means that you'll be working on your own. People often think that a dissertation should be 'original', which implies that the topic has never been done before. Don't panic! This is not the case. Examiners are simply looking for evidence that you're capable of researching, analysing evidence and constructing texts by yourself, independent of external structures of support.

Research

In the past, you may have researched an author you'd been studying in class to provide you with more information about them and their text: you'd probably only have looked for information which would substantiate your initial thoughts.

In a dissertation, you'll be expected to evaluate and critically analyse different points of view connected with the texts you have chosen. It's from skilfully considering these differing points of view, that you'll probably begin to crystallise your own opinion and view point. It's important that you have confidence in your own ability to criticise as well as agree. This is where your oral discussion skills will help you.

Primary and secondary sources

These are terms you will encounter frequently when working on a dissertation. The primary sources are the texts themselves – novels, plays or poems – that you have chosen to study for your dissertation. A secondary source is a work which can provide additional information about the primary source such as biographies, literary criticism and review articles. A compelling dissertation will maintain a sound balance between the two sources. While secondary sources are useful for starting up possible new streams of reflection and research, they should never be allowed to overshadow your primary ones. The latter, after all, are the focus of your dissertation.

contd

Dissertation: What are you being asked to do?

Taking notes

You will be used to taking notes for both English and most of your other subjects. Some of you will take copious notes; others minimal. At this point in your school career, you will have developed a method which works for you.

However, with a dissertation you are essentially on your own, and you'll also be juggling the primary texts and the secondary sources. It's therefore vital that, from the outset, you devise a method of keeping track of your notes. Whatever method you adopt, you should be very careful never to lose sight of the primary texts and not to overburden yourself with information from secondary sources.

Always keep in mind that, in a dissertation, you are forming your own views and you should not become too dependent on the views of others.

Presentation style

The language of your dissertation has much in common with that of an argumentative or discursive essay. The vocabulary should be formal, with your claims well-supported by textual evidence. This evidence should be clearly linked to references in your bibliography. This you will append to the completed dissertation. It should follow a standard documentation style such as those on pages 38–39.

These elements of academic style are frequently termed, especially by universities and colleges, the 'scholarly' aspects of writing. Don't be put off by this. It just implies that you'll be 'moving up a gear' in terms of your writing and, in reality, preparing yourself for what you'll be expected to produce in the future, whatever course of academic study you choose.

Timescale

When you've written essays on novels, poems or plays previously, you'll probably have been required to do so in a set time. In N5 and Higher this will have been under exam conditions. With the dissertation, you'll still have set times in terms of deadlines, but the major difference is that this is a substantial piece of writing. You will be writing, editing and redrafting it over several months.

A convincing dissertation is the result of a long process. The outcome must demonstrate to examiners that you've acquired not only the skills to conduct independent critical research and analysis, but also the skill to write in a way which foregrounds effectively – and accurately – your detailed knowledge and understanding of the texts you've chosen. So, you see, a good dissertation cannot be 'thrown together' at the last minute.

DON'T FORGET

Learning how to research and construct a compelling dissertation for Advanced Higher English is an invaluable academic skill which you'll be able to transfer to many other academic subjects.

ONLINE

Although dissertation topics will vary depending on the subject you're studying – and there could be a variation in the way the information is presented – the process is essentially the same. You might find it useful to look at some of the general guides provided by universities and colleges. Check out the example on the Digital Zone.

THINGS TO DO AND THINK ABOUT

The final decision on your area of research is still some way off; your dissertation's title is an even more distant prospect. However, now is a good time to open up a file listing writers whose work you've enjoyed or genres of literature which have given you pleasure.

With a partner (preferably one who's also doing Advanced Higher English) discuss what it was that attracted you to these writers or works. Was it a certain theme, sense of place, or the portrayal of strong characters? Discussions of this kind, and the notes you make as you go along, can help crystallise this elusive topic.

DISSERTATION
FINDING A TOPIC

READING

A starting point

Brainstorming your initial ideas with a friend, and your teacher, is the most effective starting point. Initially, you'll probably be drawn to the authors and texts you've studied before. Although there's nothing essentially wrong with this, remember, the world is your oyster. It's good to listen to what others have enjoyed in the same genre and begin to read what they recommend. Other places to look are your school or local libraries. Librarians have a wealth of knowledge which you can tap into.

This time spent reading, thinking and talking to others is invaluable. Don't worry if you can't find a text or texts immediately: this implies that, when you do choose, you'll really want to research and write about your chosen texts.

Classic mistakes

At this stage in the process of writing a dissertation, the temptation is to attempt to formulate a title and start researching it. But, the formulation of an effective title comes with time. By all means, have a rough idea in terms of what you'd like to write about and then begin to read around the topic.

A voyage of discovery

For example, you may have enjoyed reading and studying *The Strange Case of Dr Jekyll and Mr Hyde* for Higher – particularly, the duality of the main character. Although you can't use this text, having studied it with a teacher, you could begin to explore the concept of the moral ambiguity which these characters portray.

If you really enjoyed the works of Stevenson, you could perhaps begin to read or re-read *Kidnapped* and *The Master of Ballantrae*. In your reading, you could well come across the term 'doppelgänger'. If you wished to explore this in more detail, and want to keep a Scottish element, you could go on to read *The Private Memoirs and Confessions of a Justified Sinner* by James Hogg, *Aiding and Abetting* by Muriel Spark on *The Bad Sister* by Emma Tennant. If you're not so keen on a purely Scottish-based dissertation, you could explore *A Wizard of Earthsea* by Ursula Le Guin. As you begin to read and explore, you'll find lots of avenues opening up to you.

contd

Dissertation: Finding a topic

A wild goose chase

Sometimes when you are reading with a specific, as opposed to a general, idea in your head, you'll keep reading in the vain hope that you'll find texts, characters, scenes or incidents to justify the idea that you have formulated. You may feel as though you're slogging through the reading. If this begins to happen, it's important to stop and re-evaluate your initial idea. At this point you may feel that the time you've spent reading has been wasted – it has not. You've been able to reject your idea. In all probability, such an idea would not have produced an effective dissertation.

It's important to recognise that nothing is set in stone: you can change your mind. However, this is only realistic if you start reading very early in the course.

STRATEGIES FOR READING

Feeling overwhelmed

All this reading can initially seem quite daunting. Keep in mind that writing a dissertation is a process and you are moving onto the next stage. Also, in recent years, you've been reading a wider variety of texts and more academic texts. You may now need to concentrate more on what you're reading than you have in the past. At this stage, you don't want to find yourself compelled to read everything in case you miss anything, especially with secondary sources. You only want to read the relevant sections. So, what do you do?

Techniques

You employ the techniques which you've, perhaps even subconsciously, been using for years – skimming and scanning. However, at this level you must also consider the following because you'll be making notes at the same time.

Question – Is what you are reading going to be useful to you?

Recall – Once you have read the section, can you remember any of it?

Review – Read it over again, this time making notes. Keep thinking about the relevance of what you're reading, and if what you've read has given you any new ideas to follow up.

It's at this point, when you're beginning to formulate in your mind the main area you'd like to write about, that you might find it useful to read around the subject. You'll find that you can't separate the work from the author or from the time in which it was written. For example, if you were thinking about writing about the duality of characters in the works of Robert Louis Stevenson, you would find it useful to find out about his own life and how his experiences influenced his writing. Also – because his works aren't contemporary – finding out what was happening in Scotland at the time they were written could provide useful insight into the events that his characters experienced. When you're tackling this type of reading, there's no need to take notes, just enjoy the experience.

 THINGS TO DO AND THINK ABOUT

Now, you need to stop and reflect on where you are. This would be a good time to discuss your reading and thoughts with your teacher or a friend. Thinking and discussion at this stage are essential if you want to avoid problems later on. Always keep an open mind when others make suggestions and be flexible in terms of perhaps changing or adapting your initial thoughts in light of their suggestions.

DON'T FORGET

Whatever happens with your initial reading, it's important that you begin to become an active reader who thinks about the subject. This will pay dividends when you move on to further study and are presented with extensive reading lists for perhaps more than one subject.

 ONLINE

For some handy questions to keep in mind while you're reading around, head to the Digital Zone.

 **DON'T FORGET**

It's important that when you start the next stage of the process – note-taking – that you do so with a clearer sense of purpose.

DISSERTATION

TAKING NOTES (PART 1)

Now that you've been reading around and have begun to firm up your ideas about what you'd like to write about, it's only natural that you'll want to begin to take notes on what you've been reading. It's also only natural you will assume that, because you've been making notes for years in various subjects, this part of the process will cause few problems. While this is true to an extent, there are traps which you don't want to fall into.

ORGANISATION

The key to effective note-taking for a long piece of academic writing is organisation. In the case of your dissertation, you'll be dealing with both primary and secondary sources. For novels, short stories or plays, this could amount to two or even more primary sources: if you choose poetry, you could be dealing with six or more poems. And, because you've been reading around your chosen subject, you could be dealing with perhaps three or more secondary sources. Such a situation will produce a lot of information.

Colour coding

Colour coding texts and, as will be discussed later, the different areas of your dissertation, is a fairly simple but quick way of helping you find what you're looking for. If you know what the colour signifies – note this down at the time you introduce a colour – it can really help you to find your way around your notes. But be careful not to overdo it. (This method of note-taking is also extremely useful when you're preparing your notes for the literary study.)

Quality not quantity

One of the main traps students can fall into is producing too many notes. This may happen because you're essentially on your own for the first time and you're afraid you'll miss or forget something. Notes which are too copious produce their own problems. You could find yourself in a situation where can't see the wood for the trees. In other words, you've so many notes, you lose sight of the key/relevant points.

Primary sources

A major difference between making notes that you can use effectively to write your dissertation (and those which you would make for other subjects) is the importance placed by examiners on quotations from, or references to, the primary sources that you have chosen to write about – the novels, plays or poems. There's always the temptation that, once you've read, annotated and analysed your chosen texts, you focus on the opinions expressed in the secondary sources rather than those expressed in the primary sources.

Evidence

It's essential that you provide some good evidence and reasons for the opinions and views that you put forward. For example, there's no good writing down in your notes that Tennessee Williams employed colour symbolism in his play *A Streetcar Named Desire* if you've no evidence to back it up. If you did this, you would be making an assertion without any grounds for it. All this would tell the examiner is that you know the technical name for symbolism.

While searching for evidence of colour symbolism, make sure your notes contain page references. This will save you a lot of time when you come to the writing-up process. We'll cover how to use the evidence you've gathered most effectively in *The Craft of Writing* (parts 1 and 2).

contd

Dissertation: Taking notes (part 1)

Secondary sources

While it must be acknowledged that secondary sources are useful, you should not rely too heavily on them.

Summarising

When you're reading secondary sources and starting to make notes, it's vital that you summarise in your own words, as far as possible, what point the author is making. You'll find that this will not only help you remember the points being made, but it will help you avoid plagiarism.

Summarising should also help you to pick out only those quotations you think will be useful. (And, remember, use quotation marks for these even in your notes!)

Plagiarism

A dissertation should be your own work. Plagiarism can sometimes be accidental. This is why it's a good idea, as outlined above, to summarise in your own words, the point which is being made. If you're in a rush to finish – something that shouldn't happen if you've kept to the deadlines set by your teacher – you may include verbatim something you've noted down without acknowledging the source.

Remember that most examiners have an extensive knowledge of literature and could well spot plagiarism if you've used specific keywords that are either being used out of context, are not in keeping with your own style of writing, or the original author expressed them in such a way that the examiner has remembered them.

DON'T FORGET

It's essential that you always include in your notes – especially of secondary sources – the title, author and page number. Not only in case you want to revisit the point later within its original context, but also for inclusion in your Bibliography. Even at the note-taking stage, it's useful to open a Bibliography file where you can note down all of your primary and secondary sources. The method you'll use will be discussed later in the Creating a bibliography section on pages 38–39.

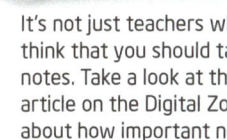

ONLINE

It's not just teachers who think that you should take notes. Take a look at the article on the Digital Zone about how important note-taking is to further study, and indeed, in all walks of life.

 THINGS TO DO AND THINK ABOUT

Once you've made a few notes, it's worthwhile reviewing how productive and effective those notes will be. To do this, try to answer the following questions:

- Can I reduce what I've written?
- Why have I written this down?
- Could I begin to use keywords to express ideas?
- Can I use this point to make any connections with other ideas?

You could also use this method of reviewing and reflecting to help you revise for the Literary Study element of the exam.

DISSERTATION

TAKING NOTES (PART 2)

AN EXAMPLE

Imagine that you're thinking about characters in two plays by Tennessee Williams. You could be focusing on *A Streetcar Named Desire* (if you hadn't studied it for Higher) and *Cat on a Hot Tin Roof*.

One of your ideas may be concerned with characters who cannot face reality. This is what your notes might look like.

Streetcar

CHARACTER/QUOTE	COMMENT	SECONDARY SOURCE
Blanche Dubois – 'I never was hard or self sufficient enough … If you're going to have someone's protection.' (p.169)	Southern Belle – lost Belle Reve but it did not really provide her with what she wanted. Her world has collapsed and she has to learn to survive	Williams shows the decline of the southern gentry through the lives of its daughters. 'Truth and illusion in Tennessee Williams' A Streetcar Named Desire' esnbu.org/data/files/2016/ 2016-1-6-gencheva-pp31-41.pdf by A Gencheva - Related articles
'Life has to go on. No matter what happens, you've got to keep going.' (neighbour p.217)	For Blanche to survive she has to resort to wilful invention. She is defending her own constructions.	Idea of despair breeding hope and then the idea of hope collapsing into despair. Jackson, E. M. 'The Broken World of Tennessee Williams'
'I don't want realism … I want Magic … I tell what ought to be the truth.' (p.203–204) '… soft people have got to count on the favour of hard ones … shimmer and grow' (p.92)	Another example of her survival strategies. Consider how we would react.	
'After all a woman's charm is 50% illusion.' (p.129)	Blanche turns to sexual promiscuity. She believes that women should create an illusion.	
'I was flirting with your husband.' (p.141) 'I have old fashioned ideals' (p.198) and 'Flamingo incident'	Audience not surprised – already know that she is not what she appears to be on the surface – drinking etc.	

contd

Dissertation: Taking notes (part 2)

Now move on to think about the next of your chosen plays, *Cat on a Hot Tin Roof*.

This time in your notes, include any points of comparison or contrast.

Cat

CHARACTER/QUOTES	COMMENTS	COMPARE AND CONTRAST WITH STREETCAR
Brick – wearing white silk pyjamas 'Will you just put on a pair of white silk pyjamas?' (p.30)	Sexuality introduced from the beginning – Brick fending off Maggie's amorous advances.	Stanley dressed 'in brilliant silk pyjamas' (p.214) makes Blanche the 'Tiger' drop the bottle top, but in Cat sexual assault reduced to a gesture.
And 'Seizes a small boudoir chair and raises it like a lion tamer.' (p.31)	This is where he attempts to return to the real world and it fails.	Blanche and Brick both retreat from the real world. Blanche's life was never the dream she pretended it was.
'I was running and jumping the hurdles and they got too high for me.' (p.53)	Brick's dream life is over.	Blanche – the end, Brick – the beginning.
He tells his father he no longer 'believes'. (p.74) – some discussion of this – several quotes.		In both plays – suicide has aborted a marriage. Exposure and eviction are devastating in Streetcar – only idle threats in Cat.
Secondary Sources		
For Williams, the homosexuality in Cat was 'a relationship which must have involved a tenderness which was uncommon'. Bigsby, C. W. E. (Ed.) (1982) *A Critical Introduction to Twentieth Century American Drama*, Cambridge, Cambridge University Press		

 **DON'T FORGET**

Always keep in mind when you're making notes that they shouldn't be so detailed that you end up 'making notes on your notes'. The purpose of making notes is to help you formulate and crystallise your ideas so that you can move forward to the next stage in the process.

 ## THINGS TO DO AND THINK ABOUT

Now that you've made your initial notes, talk about them with a partner. This will help you to clarify how useful they're going to be. If you're giving feedback to your partner, try to be constructive.

DISSERTATION
THINKING OF TOPICS AND TITLES

Now that you've made some notes, reviewed them and discussed them with your teacher and/or a partner, a topic should be beginning to form in your mind. You could, of course, have gone through the process of thinking of something and then rejecting it several times – at this early stage, there's nothing unusual in this. The more time you spend thinking about things, the more likely you are to ultimately succeed.

A CASE STUDY

Once you've decided upon a topic you feel happy with – and importantly feel you'll enjoy writing about – do NOT immediately rush to think of a title.

The most effective way to tackle this is to review your notes and very briefly write down the key points. This will allow you to see even more clearly how your mind was working when you were making the notes.

If, for example, you had been looking at four novels by E. M. Forster – *A Room with a View*, *Where Angels Fear to Tread*, *A Passage to India* and *Howard's End* – you will have realised that, although all four have strong female characters, attempting to write about four novels would be far too difficult within the word limit. In fact, you wouldn't be able to do justice to all the work you'll have done.

How do you decide?

Write down the key points about each of the female characters on a page.

Which two or three do you feel most comfortable with?

You could decide on two: *A Room with a View* and *Where Angels Fear to Tread*.

Here's what your list of key points for these novels might look like:

A Room with a View – Lucy Honeychurch	Where Angels Fear to Tread – Caroline Abbott
Lucy changes because of her travels and experiences	Caroline changes because of her travels and experiences
Setting – Italy	Setting – Sawston, Italy
Influence of beauty and freedom	Influence of beauty and freedom
Lucy – confused	Caroline – trapped
Influence of society – men – George Emerson	Influence of society – men – Gino
Lucy – sees the view/idea of light not darkness	Caroline – understands life

How this helps

What emerges from this is both female characters find themselves in situations they are not familiar with, and neither really understands what's happening to them.

It would be very difficult to try to write down a title from this, so, the most effective thing you can do is write yourself a note:

contd

18

Dissertation: Thinking of topics and titles

I would like to examine – perhaps compare – the novels *A Room with a View* and *Where Angels Fear to Tread* by E. M. Forster.

Each of these novels has a strong female character who is out of her depth – because of something which she experiences.

Each of the characters finds that she has no support from the middle-class society she is accustomed to.

Comment on the result for both characters.

Important – my comparison must be detailed and I must concentrate on the literary and/or linguistic aspects – I must NOT focus on the respective narratives.

 **DON'T FORGET**

Remember that this is a work in progress at this stage; you can still make changes.

 THINGS TO DO AND THINK ABOUT

Discussion is a vital part of the process of writing any dissertation or academic essay. With a partner, read the example 'summaries' of possible dissertations. While you're reading them, make a few notes on how the summaries could be improved to make the topic more workable – considering the following questions will help you to do this. Although you may not know all the texts, you should be able to get a 'feel' for what will work and what will not.

- Is the topic very narrow or too broad to produce an in-depth study?
- Is there the possibility of effecting a detailed comparison?
- Is the topic sufficiently demanding for this level of study?
- Is there an opportunity to focus on literary and or linguistic features?
- Is there a danger of excessive reliance on secondary sources?
- Are the works selected of reasonable literary quality?

Example 1:
The concept of Grace is central to Flannery O'Connor's preoccupation with the impact of religion on society and its influence on human behaviour. I intend to discuss, making close reference to her novels and short stories, her portrayal of this concept and my reaction to it.

Example 2:
A comparative literary study of the themes of division and reconciliation in the novels *Where Angels Fear to Tread*, *A Room with a View* and *A Passage to India* by E. M. Forster.

Example 3:
A study of a selection of the religious poems of T. S. Eliot.

Example 4:
A critical study of *The Four Quartets* by T. S. Eliot. There will be a careful analysis of the language and imagery and how they are used to isolate Eliot's central themes and concerns. There will be an attempt to show his emergence from his earlier pessimism into a form of hope.

Example 5:
An exploration of the theme of social suppression and the way in which the characters struggle to gain freedom in the plays *A Doll's House*, *Hedda Gabler* and *The Lady from the Sea*. There will be an evaluation of how successfully this is conveyed using a variety of literary devices such as symbolism and irony. There will also be a comparison of Ibsen's style and approach to these at different times in his career.

Example 6:
An examination of the portrayal of marital relations between the two main characters in the plays *Cat on a Hot Tin Roof* by Tennessee Williams, *Who's Afraid of Virginia Wolf* by Edward Albee and *Look Back in Anger* by John Osborne. There will be an exploration of how the development of characters within the marital relationships is used to highlight the playwrights' central themes.

 **DON'T FORGET**

You may be tempted to write about only one text, but this could be risky. The text would need to be seriously substantial in order to produce the same depth and breadth that a dissertation on more than one text would produce.

DISSERTATION
PLANNING

The dissertation should be between 2500 and 3000 words, including quotations but excluding footnotes and bibliography. (SQA)

Although you may have written what you've thought were long essays in the past – for example, your Higher Portfolio – this will probably be the first time you'll be required to write something of this length. You really need to think about the word limit **before** you start structuring your essay. You don't want to find yourself in the position of having written too much and having to cut things out, or having written too little and having to write about things you didn't intend to.

LENGTH

Now that you've decided on your topic, you must think about how you're going to write about it.

I'm sure that, in the past, one of your teachers will have commented on your work that you have wandered off the subject or that your essay was not balanced. You don't want this to happen at this stage. You have approximately 2500 words. Your dissertation, like your other essays in the past, will be made up of three main parts – the introduction, the main body and the conclusion. This is where the maths comes in.

You have roughly 200 words for each of the introduction and conclusion: these 400 words should not be used for anything else. That leaves you with about 2100 for the main body of your essay. By sticking to this, you will avoid some of the most common pitfalls – for example, writing about 750 words to introduce the dissertation before you even start to write about the topic!

DON'T FORGET

Whatever subject or topic you're writing about, think ahead if you want to avoid time-consuming problems later. Remember that no one ever knows what they're going to write about until they have actually written it. If it makes you feel more secure, draft an introduction to guide your own thoughts, but leave finalising it until you have completed your dissertation and you're happy with your conclusion. You don't want to arouse expectations in your examiner's mind and then not satisfy them!

CONTENT

By the time you reach this stage, you'll have organised your notes using the method you are most comfortable with. You may have colour coded them, used diagrams, charted the information or arranged your ideas on cards. Whichever method you've used, you should have a list of the key points in front of you. This will allow you to see where the points of comparison and/or contrast emerge. This should then enable you to think about how much you'll write about each of your chosen texts. It would be very simple if all you had to do was divide your remaining 2100 words by either two or three and allocate the 1050 or 700 words to each of the texts.
However, this will not produce the most effective dissertation.

Dissertation: Planning

 THINGS TO DO AND THINK ABOUT

Before starting to plan for content, re-read some of your own essays from English or other subjects. These essays are likely to have been written in response to a question. Think carefully about the question you were answering and if any comments were made about the structure of the essay. You can also swap your essays with others in the class and try to answer the following questions:

- Was the structure appropriate to the question?
- Was the essay 'balanced'?
- Did you or the others wander off the subject?
- Was the question actually answered?

Make a note of what you find before giving feedback. Be prepared to justify your comments.

 ONLINE

Head to the Digital Zone to find a document outlining the criteria for the Advanced Higher English course.

Dissertation

STRUCTURING

DON'T FORGET

This won't apply if you're writing about only one substantial text. However, you'd need to illustrate an element of complexity in the structuring of such a dissertation.

DON'T FORGET

It's important to keep thinking of the dissertation as a process comprised of many stages. Sometimes, in a fit of frustration, we crumple up our planning sheets and aim them at the nearest bin. Don't. There may be something there that you'll want to refer to in future.

DON'T FORGET

Always be open minded and flexible in your approach. Pursuing a line of thought which you begin to realise is not going as 'planned' is pointless and will not produce a good dissertation.

THE COMPARATIVE ELEMENT

Although it may seem strange, one of the last things you'll write will be your introduction. This is because the introduction must provide a clear indication of what will be written about – and we can all wander off the subject. This can only be achieved when you've written the main body of the dissertation.

What you must focus on at this stage is the comparative element. Writing about two or more texts is a more complex process than writing about one. While it's easier – especially if you're under pressure and writing up your dissertation at the last minute – to simply write about one text and then the other, try to link them together in the conclusion. This is true comparative writing.

By being well prepared, using your notes and taking your time, you'll soon develop the skills of weaving together your ideas and arguments about your chosen texts.

CONNECTIONS AND CONTRASTS

Connections

By making notes of each text's key points, you have, in fact, already started to clarify your ideas and make **connections**. Keep reviewing your notes to ensure you're clear about any similarities between the texts. Here, you can begin to explore those similarities in more detail, using quotations from your primary sources and any comments from your secondary sources. (This is where having written down the page numbers is particularly useful.)

A case study

Think about a dissertation focusing on a comparative study of how the writers characterise the motivation and moral values of the protagonists in *No Mean City* by A. McArthur and H. Kingsley Long and *Laidlaw* by William McIlvanney.

To begin with, note that this is a comparative study – so you would expect there to be points both of comparison and contrast.

At first glance, these two novels appear to have much in common and probably little in the way of contrast. (This may be why you initially chose them.) You'd then start by attempting to make connections between them, hoping that the contrasts will emerge as you explore those connections. If they don't, consider changing your topic slightly.

Using the key points idea, your initial notes would look something like this:

KEY POINT	NO MEAN CITY	LAIDLAW
Violence and the factors which motivate aggression.	Johnnie Stark and McLatchie, a rival gang leader, taking part in an arranged fight in front of 'a crowd numbering close upon a thousand …' on Glasgow Green. (p.123) Fight turns into a riot – razors appear.	John Rhodes is a kind of local 'godfather' figure. People are afraid of him. 'The blue eyes turned on him like a blow torch lit but not yet shooting a flame.' (p.116)
The need to live up to reputation.	This illustrates the uncompromising brutality, typical of Johnnie.	

contd

Dissertation: Structuring

Motivations which underpin their lives are buried under various assumptions about the way of life in that part of the world.	Johnnie's vanity is shown by the fact that, in his teenage years, he trains on the Green to keep his body in shape and he doesn't like people to see him defeated in battle – 'Vanity is as much a dominant motive in the slums as outside them. Johnnie had little to be proud of except his strong body and his reckless spirit'. (p.28)	Laidlaw has a big ego. Drinking in a police bar in Glasgow after a dressing down by his commander, Laidlaw is approached by a gloating Milligan – 'Does it ever cross your mind … because you're right. I wouldn't forget'. (p.224)
Do not display emotions.	Johnnie, after his mother's death, turns up at her funeral to see her in her coffin. He stands over it and obviously feels great emotion but is determined not to display it in case people thought him soft – 'Johnnie stood for a moment … terrified lest any present should detect in him any sign of weakness or sentiment'. (p.160)	Bud Lawson, the father of the murdered teenager Jenner, is typical of this. On hearing the news, he doesn't speak but resorts to drinking whisky instead – 'Slowly the whisky had played upon their grouped moods until their anger found expression'. (pp. 8–9)
Accepted cultures of the area – football, gambling, religious bigotry and especially alcohol.	Most of Johnnie's attacks are fuelled by alcohol. In the Gorbals, it was accepted that this is what men did. 'Johnnie had just enough drink in him that night to make him entirely reckless of the consequences.' (p.132)	Laidlaw has very little life outside of work and spends a lot of his time drinking. Bud Lawson and the other men start to talk about revenge once the alcohol takes over their minds (see quote above from pp. 8–9)

DON'T FORGET

When making notes like this, it's always easier to start with the same novel for each key point. This helps you to organise your work and better structure your dissertation.

DON'T FORGET

Remember, when comparing texts, it's unlikely you'll be able to produce a balanced dissertation in terms of connections and contrasts.

Contrasts

When you've done this, you can move on to think about any contrasts that have become apparent. Sometimes these only emerge when you examine the connections in detail. As you begin to reflect on the connections you've made between the two novels, your initial notes on the contrasts – again using the key points idea – would look something like this.

KEY POINT	NO MEAN CITY	LAIDLAW
Genre	Although fictional, it describes life in the Gorbals in documentary detail. It presents an extended contrast between Johnnie Stark, trapped in the cycle of Gorbals life, and Peter Stark and Bobbie Hurley, ambitious to make their escape from it.	A crime thriller written in a style typical of the genre.
Style	Limited in style because the book was ghost written by a journalist and most of the narration and description is clichéd. '… his bleeding lips were parted in an animal snarl. Like an animal he roared as he sprang at two young fellows…' (p.152). This journalistic style can intrude on the narrative.	McIlvanney's typical pacy, gritty narrative style. He deliberately makes the characters larger than life. A more literary style with frequent use of figurative language. He has a good ear for the Glasgow 'patter'. 'Say ye could get yer hands on who did it. Surmisin' like. Whit wid ye do? Ah'd kill 'im.' (p.190)

Of course, these are simply examples and they would need to be 'fleshed out' and more quotations found to illustrate the points.

THINGS TO DO AND THINK ABOUT

Choose two extracts from your chosen texts, or, in the case of poetry, two poems. Using the key points method, or whichever method works for you, write as fully as you can about the connections and contrasts between the two texts. Swap with a partner, make some notes, and discuss your feedback together.

DISSERTATION

STRUCTURING AND LINKAGE

In the main body of your dissertation, you will be developing your argument by using your own ideas and opinions, and quotations from primary and secondary sources. You're working through the key points you have made and supporting them with evidence.

ONLINE

Check out the section on 'the main body' of a dissertation in the article on the Digital Zone.

DON'T FORGET

You must always try to interweave your texts. Don't write about them separately and then try to draw them together in the conclusion.

MAIN BODY

How you structure the main body of your dissertation will depend on the texts you've chosen and the line of thought you're trying to develop. From the case studies in the other sections, you'll be able to see how a structure begins to emerge.

A CASE STUDY

If you've chosen to write about only two texts, the structure can be relatively straightforward to formulate. However, if you've chosen to write about several poems, it can be far more complex and you still must stick to the word limit.

Think about a dissertation which focuses on an investigation of the way in which Sylvia Plath uses colour symbolism in a selection of her poems – 'Tulips', 'Elm', 'Nick and the Candlestick', 'The Moon and the Yew Tree', 'Daddy' and 'Lady Lazarus'.

As with novels or drama, you would use your key points to help structure your dissertation.

Your initial notes could look something like the table on the left.

POEM	COLOUR
Tulips	Red, white
Elm	Red
Lady Lazarus	Red
Edge	White, black
Nick and the Candlestick	White, yellow, red, black
The Moon and the Yew Tree	Blue, black
Daddy	Black

As you can see, there's a predominance of certain colours in particular poems. Instead of discussing each poem individually, the colours can be used as the basis of the structure – thus, interweaving the poems.

Linkage

As you already know from your work on the Higher Portfolio, linking your paragraphs is of great importance to the overall flow and readability of an essay.

To achieve an effective interweaving of several poems, such as those outlined above, the topic and last sentences of the respective paragraphs or sections are extremely important.

As with all essay writing after the introduction, the topic sentence of the first paragraph should provide a clear link back to the topic being written about, as well as an indication of how you're going to develop your ideas.

Section 1

> The use of colours as a symbol is perhaps most evident in 'Tulips', where the redness of the flowers is a vivid symbol of pain, as in the lines:
>
> 'The tulips are too red … they hurt me.'

The remainder of the section would discuss the use of the colour red in 'Elm', where it is associated with danger, heat and anger and 'Lady Lazarus', where it is a symbol of strength and life – more positive connotations. The last sentence of such a paragraph could possibly highlight this:

> In this poem ['Lady Lazarus'], red relates to fire and blood, symbolising life and vitality, which contrasts with its use as a symbol for pain and danger in the other poems.

contd

Dissertation: Structuring and linkage

Section 2

Returning to your initial table of key points, you could now discuss her use of the colour white, once again starting with 'Tulips'.

> In 'Tulips' the symbolism of red is particularly effective when set against the whiteness of the hospital walls and sheets, which represents peacefulness and numbness.

In the remainder of this section, there could be a discussion of the idea that Plath only uses red and white in 'Tulips' but in 'Edge' she uses white and black to represent the innocence of the woman's children and death respectively. Also, in 'Nick and the Candlestick', she moves from white, through yellow to red and then to black, reflecting the changing mood and atmosphere of the poem. As in the paragraph above, the last sentence could attempt to highlight the contrast between the use of colour in 'Nick and the Candlestick' and the other poems:

> 'Let the stars
> Plummet to their dark address.'
>
> Here, the blackness echoes the 'Black bat airs' in the second stanza and emphasises the mother's inner thoughts: her worries and suffering are returning.

Section 3

To avoid a mechanistic approach, an effective link could be established here using the idea of Plath using colour to indicate inner thoughts. At this stage in the dissertation, you should also be establishing links back to what you've already written.

> In 'The Moon and the Yew Tree' Plath also deals with inner thoughts. The images of coldness and darkness in 'Nick and the Candlestick' are echoed in the first two lines which contain similar colour imagery:
>
> 'This is the light of the mind, cold and planetary
> The trees of the mind are black. The light is blue'

The focus for the remainder of this section would be on the use of black in the poems 'The Moon and the Yew Tree', 'Nick and the Candlestick' and 'Daddy'. Black is the dominant colour in 'Daddy' and so ending this section on this poem would be appropriate. You would now be nearing the end of the main body of the dissertation and so this would be an opportunity to pull all the different strands together:

> Throughout 'Daddy' Plath uses the colour black to highlight the intense pain and great hatred she had towards her father. The impact of the poem is effectively described by Elizabeth Hardwick when she writes:
>
> 'You cannot read it without shivering. All the hatred in our own hearts find its unforgiving music there.'[1]

[1] Hardwick, E. (1974) *Seduction and Betrayal: Women in Literature*, London, Random House, p. 115

How this helps

By thinking about interweaving your texts at the planning stage, you will avoid the 'guided tour' approach to your dissertation.

 THINGS TO DO AND THINK ABOUT

Review the key points that you've made about connections and contrasts between the texts you have chosen. This should give you the basis of your sections of the dissertation. Now review each section individually and make notes on how you could begin and end each section. Discussion is always useful. By justifying your ideas to a partner, you'll begin to see how interweaving can be achieved.

 DON'T FORGET

Interweaving the texts – no matter how many you're writing about – is essential. By adopting an approach like the one outlined on this page, you will avoid the pitfall of simply writing about one text and then another.

 ONLINE

You'll find some interesting articles online about the way in which Plath used colour in her poetry. One such site can be found via the Digital Zone.

Dissertation

INTRODUCTIONS – CASE STUDIES (PART 1)

After looking at your title, your introduction is the first thing that your examiner will read. Depending on what you're writing about, an introduction can do several things. The main ones, however, are:

- to outline what you are going to write about
- to provide an indication of your line of thought or argument.

People often include:

- a relevant quotation to get the examiner's attention
- any biographical information relevant to the topic.

A simple way to think about an introduction is as a sat nav. Your examiner is going to follow the information that you input into it so that they arrive at the destination you want them to. You'll not only be telling them what your intended destination is, but the route you are going to take to get there and why you have chosen it, any places you're going to stop at on the way, and if there are any places to avoid.

If you think about an introduction in this way, it will indicate to your examiner that you've understood what you're going to be writing about, and that you can think in an ordered and logical way.

WHEN TO WRITE YOUR INTRODUCTION

All of this implies that you must write your introduction first, but you don't have to. Many students spend a long time before they start writing the main body of their dissertations, questioning every word they have included in their introductions. This is pointless.

Before you start to write, you should have a clear idea in your head of what you're going to be writing about, but you should simply draft an introduction and move on to the main body of your dissertation. After all, you may start out thinking that you're going to follow your notes to the letter but, as you write, you could discover that you're quite naturally developing a point in a way you had not thought of at the planning stage. There's nothing wrong with this.

In fact, the ideal time to write your introduction is when you have finished writing your dissertation. This may sound strange but sometimes, when you plan a route to your destination, you can come across a diversion that your sat nav hadn't indicated.

So, always check your introduction against the contents of your dissertation. Have you written about what you wanted to write about? Have you added in something you had not thought about? Do you need to remove a few things here and there? Do you need to reset your sat nav to take your examiner to a different destination?

DON'T FORGET

Learning how to construct and review an introduction for Advanced Higher English is an invaluable academic skill which you will be able to transfer to many other academic subjects.

CASE STUDIES

Now that you've revised the purpose of an introduction, it's worthwhile looking at a few in more detail.

In the previous case studies, four different topics for possible dissertations were discussed – focusing on the works of Tennessee Williams, E. M. Forster, H. Long Kingsley and William McIlvanney and Sylvia Plath respectively. It would now be useful to look at possible introductions to some of these topics.

Here are some questions to think about while we do this.

contd

Is the topic being written about clear from the introduction? Can you follow it? Is it too brief? Are the texts mentioned? Have a close look at the style of writing – is the vocabulary basic or sophisticated? What about the sentence structure – is it simple or complex? Is there a variety of sentence structures? Are there any relevant and interesting quotations? Does it grab your attention and stand out?

DRAMA – WRITING INTRODUCTIONS

Tennessee Williams

At the note-taking stage, there was a focus on characters in three plays by Tennessee Williams – 'You could be focusing on the two plays, *A Streetcar Named Desire* (if you had not studied it for Higher) and *Cat on a Hot Tin Roof*. After exploring this general topic in more detail, it could be developed into something more specific such as:

'An examination of the dramatic techniques Tennessee Williams uses to create characters who are isolated from their families and society because they are unable to face the truth about themselves. Particular reference will be made to *A Streetcar Named Desire* and *Cat on a Hot Tin Roof*.

Here is a possible introduction – let's see what you make of it.

> During the 1940s and 1950s, Tennessee Williams helped to initiate a transformation in American drama. He introduced harsh, realistic subjects, often with shocking topics such as rape and homosexuality. His plays deal mainly with a consistent theme – self-pity – and a memory which holds people in its grip and refuses to allow them to carry on with their lives. In many of his plays, Williams wrote about characters who were isolated from their families and society, unable to face the truth about themselves. He called these characters 'my little company of the faded and the frightened, the difficult, the odd and the lonely'. They were people who battled with their personal demons against the modern world. In this dissertation, I propose to examine the dramatic techniques that Williams uses to create these characters. I will make particular reference to *A Streetcar Named Desire* and *Cat on a Hot Tin Roof*.

Williams, T. (1962) 'A Streetcar Named Desire and Other Plays', London, Penguin

Let's look at the positives and negatives of such an introduction:

POSITIVES	NEGATIVES
Topic is clear – texts are mentioned.	Texts are mentioned at the end – examiners like to know what texts are being written about to evaluate the introduction.
Relevant background information about the time period and the plays.	Style – sentence structure – over use of 'he'.
Relevant quotation from Tennessee Williams.	Style – use of 'I will' – stating the obvious.
Length – not too long.	

Using the information in the table, this introduction would only require a little reorganisation, and a few adjustments to the sentence structure, to become an effective one for the topic chosen.

 ONLINE

Head to the Digital Zone for some more interesting points about introductions.

 THINGS TO DO AND THINK ABOUT

Now that you are thinking about your introduction, quickly draft what you think you might include at this stage. Keep it, and compare it with the final introduction that you write. You may find it has changed. If so, this highlights the importance of writing your final version of the introduction once you have written your dissertation.

DISSERTATION

INTRODUCTIONS – CASE STUDIES (PART 2)

NOVEL – WRITING INTRODUCTIONS

H. Kingsley Long and William McIlvanney

At the note-taking stage, the focus was on a comparative study of how the writers characterise the motivation and moral values of the protagonists in *No Mean City* by A. McArthur and H. Kingsley Long and *Laidlaw* by William McIlvanney. With perhaps the inclusion of 'literary' in 'a comparative literary study', this would be an acceptable topic for a dissertation.

Here's a possible introduction:

> *No Mean City* and *Laidlaw* are both set in Glasgow. At first glance, these two novels appear to have much in common – for example, the Glasgow setting, with their powerful representations of slum environments and the effect of poverty on people's lives. However, closer reading reveals more difference than similarities.

Now, let's look at the table to the left for the positives and negatives of this introduction.

As there are clearly more negatives in this example, more work is needed. There's no mention of the focus on the protagonists; and the style it's written in, and its brevity, would not grab an examiner's attention.

POSITIVES	NEGATIVES
Titles of texts at the beginning – a clear indication of which texts are being written about.	No mention of characters.
Indication of similarities and differences – comparative element – but brief.	Comparative element – but no mention of literary aspect.
	Brief.
	Basic style – more sophisticated vocabulary, more complex sentence structure needed.

POETRY – WRITING INTRODUCTIONS

Sylvia Plath

At the note-taking stage, this dissertation was going to focus on an investigation of the way in which Sylvia Plath uses colour symbolism in a selection of her poems – 'Tulips', 'Elm', 'Nick and the Candlestick', 'The Moon and the Yew Tree', 'Daddy' and 'Lady Lazarus'.

This would be an acceptable topic if something was added to indicate that it was going to be a literary study, and that, as the candidate explored the topic, they discovered Plath used colour to symbolise her pain and suffering.

This is an example of how the focus of a dissertation can change slightly further to explore the topic and author in more detail.

What do you think of the following introduction?

> The poems in Sylvia Plath's collection *Ariel* were written during the last few years of her life, the years leading up to her infamous suicide. Her poetry of this time displays a fundamental message of anguish and despair, pain and suffering. *Ariel* can be viewed as a series of suicide notes, exploring different aspects of suffering in her life – for example, physical pain in 'Tulips'; the general cruelty of the world in 'Nick and the Candlestick'; and her relationship with her father in 'Daddy'. To communicate this sense of pain and suffering to the reader, Plath effectively uses colours. Indeed, Damian Grant has commented that Plath epitomises:
>
> 'the complicated use of colours, almost as symbolism, to signify states of mind and attitudes'.[1]
>
> Clearly, Plath achieved this.

DON'T FORGET

First impressions are important; so, your introduction needs to be good. But it must also ensure the marker is clear about your destination and how you're going to reach it.

[1] Grant, D. (1972) 'Critical Quarterly, Spring 1972', quoted in *Contemporary Literary Criticism*, Volume 1, Gale, p. 177

contd

Dissertation: Introductions – case studies (part 2)

To the right are the positives and negatives of this introduction:

Although there are no negative comments, the candidate will only be happy with it if it reflects what they have written about.

How this helps

You now know about the positive and negative aspects of introductions. You could make three or four attempts before you get it just right. Take your time.

POSITIVES	NEGATIVES
Focus of topic is clear.	
Main poems are mentioned near the beginning.	
Brief comment on each poem in light of the topic.	
Relevant quote.	
Effective style.	

THINGS TO DO AND THINK ABOUT

It's important to discuss your introduction with your teacher or a partner. You may think you've written a clear, interesting and memorable introduction, but it's good to have some confirmation. With a partner read the following example introductions to dissertations and make a few notes. Use a grid like this one to evaluate the positive and negative aspects. You may not know all the texts, but you should be able to get a 'feel' for what will and won't work.

ASPECT	POSITIVE	NEGATIVE
Topic of the dissertation		
Texts		
Vocabulary		
Style		
Relevant quotations		
Relevant background information		
Attention grabbing		

Example 1: Drama – Samuel Beckett

Consider the following topic: An examination of the treatment of time in the plays *Waiting for Godot*, *Endgame* and *Happy Days* by Samuel Beckett.

> Irving Wardle in 'New English Dramatists 12' recognises that one characteristic of the theatre of the absurd is 'a free attitude towards time, which expands or contracts according to subjective requirements'[1]. Samuel Beckett can be seen in some lights as an absurdist playwright and the aspect of time is explored in some depth in many of his plays. In this dissertation, I intend to explore Beckett's 'free attitude towards time' in the context of various theories of time, to discover his own standpoint and how that relates to the meanings of the plays. Particular reference will be made to the plays *Waiting for Godot*, *Endgame* and *Happy Days*.

[1] Wardle, I. (1968), *New English Dramatists 12*, Harmondsworth, Penguin Books.

Example 2: Novel – Graham Greene

Consider the following topic: A literary examination of the idea that religion is the result of insecurity in the works of Graham Greene, with particular reference to *Brighton Rock* and *The Power and the Glory*.

> Graham Greene has, in the past, been stereotyped by critics and readers as a Catholic novelist. Greene, however, often expressed his dislike of this description, as have many Catholics. They regard the theology in his novels with suspicion, because the think it may give non-Catholics a false impression of their beliefs. The novels discussed in this dissertation are, in the main, described as religious novels. However, I hope to reveal that his use of religion was the result of an, up till now, disregarded influence on his writing: insecurity.

Example 3: Poetry – Carol Ann Duffy

Consider the following topic: An analysis of how Carol Ann Duffy uses imagery, language and narrative voice in *Rapture* to transcend time and love itself. There will also be consideration of their contribution to the development of the portrayal of the central relationship.

> Carol Ann Duffy's *Rapture* (2005) takes the form of a love affair. It offers a unique, narrative, lyrical voice which pays close attention to repetition and word play, contributing to the development of the central relationship.
>
> Imagery of nature and the seasons permeates the anthology, linking with the idea of time and the suggestion of the transcendence of love over time. This allows for the interweaving of the rediscovery of things lost or undervalued and self-reflection. The past is linked to the present; acknowledging the debt of the of the transcendence of tradition and creating up-to-date images.

DISSERTATION

CONCLUSIONS (PART 1)

You have now reached your destination and will no doubt be breathing a sigh of relief. If everything's gone to plan, your examiner will have reached the same destination and hopefully will have had an interesting and rewarding journey.

Your conclusion will be the last thing your examiner reads and you want to end with 'a bang not a whimper'. Conclusions, like introductions, can do many things. However, in the main, they should:

- convey a sense of completion
- sum up your argument, but not go over everything again
- revisit the topic and show that you've explored it in the way you wanted
- establish a point or position relative to the topic.

People often include:

- a relevant quotation which will get the examiner's attention.

While all of this may seem obvious, there's always the temptation in a piece of work of this length to include something you forgot to include earlier. If you have a viewpoint you want to convey, the conclusion is not the place to do this: you should already have indicated it in the main body of the dissertation.

HOW TO WRITE AN EFFECTIVE CONCLUSION

You may be lucky enough to be 'on a roll' when you reach this point and, therefore, writing the conclusion will be relatively simple. However, most students find it as difficult, or even more difficult, than the introduction.

One way to tackle the problem is to review your writing and note down, on one page, the key points you have made in your topic sentences. This gives you an overview of what you've been writing about and you'll be able to check that you've included everything you needed to. Once you've done this, you should roughly draft your conclusion, and then compare it with the rough draft of your introduction.

CASE STUDY

Drama – Tennessee Williams

Here is the proposed topic:

> An examination of the dramatic techniques that Tennessee Williams uses to create characters who are isolated from their families and society because they are unable to face the truth about themselves. Particular reference will be made to *A Streetcar Named Desire* and *Cat on a Hot Tin Roof*.

Here's an improved version of the introduction we looked at earlier:

contd

Dissertation: Conclusions (part 1)

During the 1940s and 1950s, Tennessee Williams helped to initiate a transformation in American drama. He introduced harsh realistic subjects, often with shocking topics such as rape and homosexuality. His plays deal mainly with a consistent theme – self-pity – and a memory which holds people in its grip and refuses to allow them to carry on with their lives. In many of his plays, including *A Streetcar Named Desire* and *Cat on a Hot Tin Roof*, Williams wrote about characters who were isolated from their families and society, unable to face the truth about themselves. He called these characters 'my little company of the faded and the frightened, the difficult, the odd and the lonely'. They were people who battled with their personal demons against the modern world. This dissertation will examine the dramatic techniques which Williams uses to create these characters.

DON'T FORGET

However you choose to end your dissertation, your conclusion must convey a sense of completeness.

[1] Williams, T. (1962) *A Streetcar Named Desire and Other Plays*, London, Penguin

Here is a draft conclusion to this dissertation topic:

The two main characters in these plays, despite their very different lifestyles, have a vital similarity in their lives – they don't want to live in a 'real world' which does not live up to their expectations. Consequently, they withdraw into their own worlds of dreams and illusions. However, throughout the course of each play, each of these different characters finds a method of coping with reality. For Blanche in *Streetcar*, her escape from the world becomes insanity; and for Brick in *Cat*, it's compromise and joining in with a world he despises. Critics have highlighted that Williams based these characters on his own life. Like his characters, he was disillusioned by the world around him. He, like them, in the end became 'odd and lonely'.

Although perhaps not ending with a 'bang', it's not ending with a 'whimper'. It is an acceptable conclusion.

Linking conclusions with introductions

TOPIC/INTRODUCTION	CONCLUSION
Outline of topic.	Revisiting the topic. Mentions a point relevant to topic.
Mention of texts.	Mention of texts: • summary of what happens to each of the main characters in the light of the topic • in the same order as introduction.
Inclusion of biographical material.	Inclusion of biographical material.
Inclusion of relevant quotation.	Link back to relevant quotation used in introduction.
Content	It does not introduce anything new.
Length	It is about the same length as the introduction.

ONLINE

Find out more about conclusions at www.brightredbooks.net

 THINGS TO DO AND THINK ABOUT

Now that you're thinking about your conclusion, quickly draft what you might include at this stage. Keep it, and compare it with the final conclusion you write. While you're researching and writing, you may find something that you'd like to add.

DISSERTATION

CONCLUSIONS (PART 2)

Here are two possible conclusions to a dissertation on the topic of:

> An analysis of the use of opposing, yet complementary, pairs of characters as literary devices to express the moral ambiguity in the novels *The Master of Ballantrae* and *Kidnapped* by Robert Louis Stevenson.

Read through both introductions and conclusions and use the table below to help you evaluate the effectiveness of each conclusion. Remember, a conclusion must emerge out of your dissertation, not create the feeling that it's just been 'tagged on', or that you liked a specific quote and decided to include it.

CASE STUDY 1

Introduction

All men are, to a certain extent, a product of their age. Robert Louis Stevenson was no exception. Growing up in the late Victorian Age, at the zenith of the British Empire, Stevenson found himself confronted by a society which manifested a tremendous conviction and belief in its own rectitude. There was an absolute belief in the notion of Empire and an unquestioning trust in God. However, underneath this apparent moral certainty, other factors were eating away at the values of society. It is these other factors that Stevenson reflects in the novels *The Master of Ballantrae* and *Kidnapped*. The characters of James and Henry, and David and Alan reflect Stevenson's rejection of the absolute moral standards of Victorian society in favour of a more ambivalent, less rigid attitude towards 'right' and 'wrong', 'good' and 'evil'. It is the way in which Stevenson uses these characters to illustrate this which will be the focus of this dissertation.

Conclusion

There can be little doubt that Stevenson, perhaps despite himself, was writing a very different type of novel at the end of his life than the simple romance novel he championed at the outset of his writing career. People, he realised, were much more complicated than that. They presented different facets of themselves to different people at different times and in different situations. Very often, they did not know themselves and they acted instinctively, impulsively, irrationally and inconsistently. There can be little doubt that Stevenson was a psychological novelist, and little argument that, in many ways, he anticipated Freud and the repercussions his revelations were to have on the contemporary world. By reflecting the world as it really was, rather than some imaginary perfect world, he rejected the idea that good and evil are absolute values and the notion that humans can achieve moral certainty.

CASE STUDY 2

Introduction

> '… all human beings, as we know them, are commingled out of good and evil'[1]

Robert Louis Stevenson was interested in this fatal duality in human nature, and the idea that – in the soul – good and evil uncomfortably cohabit. In the works under discussion, *The Master of Ballantrae* and *Kidnapped*, he uses the literary technique of creating sets of opposing, yet complementary, characters to illustrate the moral ambiguities which result from this dichotomy.

---

[1] Stevenson, R. L. (1962) *Dr Jekyll and Mr Hyde and Other Tales*, London, Everyman, p. 51

contd

Dissertation: Conclusions (part 2)

Conclusion

It is apparent that, in the novels under discussion, absolute morality is demonstrated to be an impossibility. The two brothers in *The Master of Ballantrae*, far from representing black-and-white characters, are both flawed. James's character is dominated by a malign, manipulative and menacing presence. Henry is a victim: patient kind and unemotional. In *Kidnapped*, young David Balfour has to learn that conscience is the real arbiter of morality rather than the received values of religion or society. There are no absolutes, no moral certainties. The reader is left with a question mark of self-examination.

EVALUATING EFFECTIVENESS

Now complete the following tables for each of the case studies. Remember you can always add other headings of your own that you think would be useful to you.

Working on case study 1

TOPIC/INTRODUCTION	CONCLUSION
Awareness of topic	
Awareness of texts	
Research – biography, period in which texts were written	
Inclusion of relevant quotations	
Content – anything new or personal opinion	
Length	
Attention-grabbing bang or a whimper?	

Working on case study 2

TOPIC/INTRODUCTION	CONCLUSION
Awareness of topic	
Awareness of texts	
Research – biography, period in which texts were written	
Inclusion of relevant quotations	
Content – anything new or personal opinion	
Length	
Attention-grabbing bang or a whimper?	

THINGS TO DO AND THINK ABOUT

Now that you have some 'feel' for what makes an effective conclusion, copy and paste your introduction to the end of your dissertation. Underneath, draft a rough conclusion. By doing this you don't need to scroll up and down to check what you have written.

Using the table above, make notes on your conclusion. Now swap with a partner and provide feedback. The feedback here is vital. You must be honest with yourself and your partner because your conclusion will create a lasting impression in the mind of the examiner.

DISSERTATION

THE CRAFT OF WRITING (PART 1)

TONE AND STYLE

Being objective

Writing in an objective tone and style is something you do every day, but it can be difficult to grasp exactly what is appropriate for writing at this level. One of the easiest ways to approach this is to read some good critical reviews of texts you know well, for example, C. E. Chaffin's *T. S. Eliot: The Hollow Men*.

These texts will help you get a 'feel' for the tone and style required and give you more confidence in your writing. As well as introducing you to differing views about a text, they'll also help to raise your awareness of what is accepted language for this type of writing.

A formal tone

You can achieve the correct tone by being confident in your knowledge of your topic: the more you know, the happier you will be writing about it. A confident tone can be achieved by reading widely and thinking about how the authors have conveyed their opinions.

In the following example, the student is writing a comparative and critical analysis of the ways in which 'systems of belief' influence the creation and formulation of future societies in the novels *Brave New World* by Aldous Huxley and *Fahrenheit 451* by Ray Bradbury.

Here is a paragraph where there is a discussion about the power of advertising:

> Huxley identified advertising as one of the most influential aspects of his era. Huxley considered advertising to be, not only grotesque and vulgar, but a disturbingly powerful form of brainwashing:
>
> 'One cubic centimetre cures ten gloomy sentiments'[1]
>
> In my personal opinion, advertising was viewed by many people at this point in time, Huxley among them, as 'a direct expression of the capitalist society'[2] and 'linked with the tyranny of the machine'[3].

[1] Huxley, A. (1976) *Brave New World*, Great Britain, Longman, p. 62

[2] Calder, J. (1976) *Brave New World and Nineteen Eighty-Four: Studies in English Literature*, Southampton, Edward Arnold, p. 12

[3] Ibid

Let us now consider the tone of this extract and try to decide if it's confident or arrogant:

- Have the quotations by 'experts' been discussed or simply used as assertions?
- Do the views of the 'experts' lead to further exploration of the part of the text being discussed?
- Are there any obvious indications of assertions – for example, 'I believe' and 'In my opinion' – without any real evidence being presented?
- To what extent is the primary source the main focus of the paragraph?
- Is the point that's being made powerful and convincing?

A formal style

Reading that something should be written 'in a formal style' can initially strike fear into your heart, and then raise questions in your mind. What is a formal style?

ONLINE

Head to www.brightredbooks.net to read C.E. Chaffin's review of *T. S. Eliot: The Hollow Men* Melic Review.

DON'T FORGET

Remember that in academic writing of this type, you are exploring a topic. There will always be assumptions and an element of doubt. Although you want to be confident, you don't want to be arrogant or dogmatic.

contd

Dissertation: The craft of writing (part 1)

Here's an extract from an essay 'Blanche Dubois: An Antihero' on Tennessee Williams's *A Streetcar Named Desire* by Lauren Seigle:

> Tennessee Williams's play *A Streetcar Named Desire* presents an ambiguous moral puzzle to readers. Critics and audiences alike harbour vastly torn opinions concerning Blanche's role in the play, which range from praising her as a fallen angel victimized by her surroundings to damning her as a deranged harlot. Critic Kathleen Margaret Lant[1] claims that Williams prohibits Blanche from the realm of tragic protagonist as a result of his own culturally ingrained misogyny, using her victimization as an intentional stab at womanhood. At another end of the spectrum, critic Anca Vlasopolos[2] interprets Blanche's downfall as a demonstration of Williams's sympathy for her circumstances and a condemnation of the society that destroys her. Despite such strong convictions, debate still exists over Williams's intentions in the weaving of Blanche Dubois' tale and the purpose of the play's moral ambiguity. Throughout the play, Williams's sympathies lie with Blanche; this sympathy proves Williams is not misogynistic but rather condemns the environment that has brought about Blanche's tragic circumstances.

Marlon Brando

[1] Lant, K. M. (1991) 'A Streetcar Named Mysoginy.' in *Violence in Drama*, Cambridge, Press Syndicate of the University of Cambridge, pp. 225–238

[2] Vlasopolos, A. (1989) 'Authorizing History: Victimization in *A Streetcar Named Desire.*' in *Feminist Rereadings of Modern American Drama*, Ed. Schlueter, J., Cranbury, New Jersey, Associated University Presses, pp. 149–169

THINGS TO DO AND THINK ABOUT

It is obvious that, in the above extract, the author has adopted a formal tone and written in a formal style.

Rather than attempting to define what a formal style is, it's easier to define what should be avoided.

What to avoid

Use of the first person	Try to avoid excessive use of the first person in your dissertation. Instead of writing 'I think …' consider using expressions such as 'It is apparent that …', or 'It can be implied that …'
	The occasional use of 'I' can, however, highlight a particularly important point.
Use of colloquialisms	You will know by this time that there is a difference between formal and informal language, but the division between them is not as distinct as it once was. It is ever so easy to lapse into what you would say, rather than what you would write.
Use of abbreviations	Your writing will be more effective if you avoid abbreviated forms of formal writing such as 'didn't' and 'etc.'.
Use of numbers	Numbers should be written out in word form. For example, 6 should be written out as six. In our modern, text-orientated world we often forget this.
Use of past tense	Literary criticism, in general, is written in the present tense. For example, when writing about a scene, you would write 'the scene takes place …' not 'the scene took place …'.

ONLINE

You can find the link to Seigle's full essay at www.brightredbooks.net

DON'T FORGET

Being able to write 'in a formal style' will not happen overnight. Some fortunate people – usually those who have read widely – have an innate sense of how to write in this way. Others develop it with practice. The main aim is to communicate your ideas clearly and in an appropriate manner. Then, you'll be in control of your writing.

DISSERTATION

THE CRAFT OF WRITING (PART 2)

 **ACTIVITY**

Here is part of a draft dissertation on the literary worth of Scottish Ballads. You will see that it requires quite a lot of attention. Redraft it, improving the tone and style in as many ways as you can. Compare your version with that of a partner.

> 'The Battle of Otterbourne' is part of a group of ballads which, like Sir Patrick Spens, are fairly realistic. These ballads don't have as much depth as do more romantic ballads, e.g. 'Clerk Saunders', but I would describe them as 'thrillers' of their day. Apart from that, they are worth considering because they play a large part in the balladry of the Borders.
>
> I think that 'Otterbourne' is typical of this kind of ballad. It has all the essential ingredients of immediacy and precision right from the first verse; where the time it takes place is made clear, the hero is introduced and the story is announced:
>
> 'It fell about the Lammas tide,
>
> When the muir-men win their hay,
>
> The doughty Douglas bound him to ride
>
> Into England, to drive a prey.'[1]
>
> Now that this has my attention thus far, the story moves quickly through 'the dale of Tyne' on to 'Bambroughshire' and 'Roxburgh fells', until they come to Newcastle where the main part of the story becomes evident. What I find really interesting about this ballad is that there are lots of techniques used so that I don't get bored. The great description made me feel that I was an eyewitness to the events.

[1] www.musicanet.org/robokopp/scottish/itfellab.htm

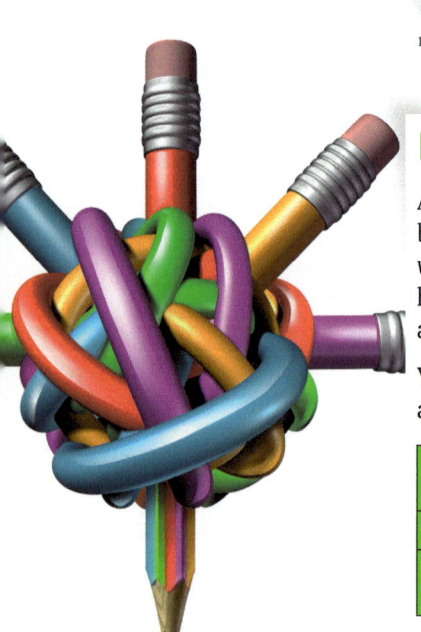

DEVELOPING YOUR OWN WRITER'S CRAFT

As your study of literature progresses, and you start on the writing process, you will begin, perhaps subconsciously, to develop an awareness of the many ways in which writers use language to achieve their aims. Effectively, critical writing does not just happen. It is something that writers think about, work very hard at and pay great attention to.

You should now be at the stage where you're able to 'craft' your own writing. Try to think about the following:

Vocabulary	Make deliberate choices: choose the most effective word, not just the first one that comes into your head.
Sentences	Vary the lengths: use different punctuation for effect.
Ideas	Think about the different ideas you want to include: weigh them up against each other when you are writing discursively.

Adding sophistication

This can be achieved through careful thought and taking your time. You don't want to fall into the trap of using lots of long and obscure words, thinking that this will impress your examiners. It will not – and is likely to have the opposite effect.

Consider the following example paragraph from a possible dissertation on the presentation of time in 'The Hollow Men' by T. S. Eliot:

contd

Dissertation: The craft of writing (part 2)

> Uni-linear time is tersely dismissed in 'The Hollow Men', where Eliot describes it using the metaphor of the London Underground: a limbo of suspended awareness in which there is no meaning in the present. There is no distinction between the past and the future and time becomes disintegrated into a meaningless sequence.

This could be written more simply as:

> In 'The Hollow Men', Eliot does not think that time is linear – as in there is the past, the present and the future. For him, time has no boundaries: it is suspended in the moment which has no meaning.

 THINGS TO DO AND THINK ABOUT

You should now be able to begin to critically evaluate your own writing – both draft and finished versions.

1. Re-read some of your own recent essays. These can be from any subject. What are the strengths and weaknesses of your written style? Think very carefully about this before you ask someone else's opinion. When you leave school, you may not always have someone else to ask, so it's a very useful skill to be able to do this for yourself.

   Choose one of the weaknesses – for example, your use of tense, or your lack of variety in sentence structure or punctuation – and rewrite some of it, trying hard to use a formal tone and style.

2. In a group of perhaps three or four, swap essays or any other form of written work. Working in pairs, read and discuss your partner's work. Consider these points:

- Is the writing easy to understand?
- Is there evidence of the use of a formal tone and style?
- Is there a variety of sentence length?
- Is there a variety of punctuation?
- Have any quotations been used effectively, not simply pasted in?

Make a note of any positive comments and advice before giving each other feedback.

 DON'T FORGET

Be careful. Crafting your own writing and adding sophistication does not mean constantly looking up a thesaurus, using elaborate comparisons, or making your sentences extremely complex. Your examiner must be able to understand what you have written and follow your line of thought. If they are distracted by the convoluted, or confusing, vocabulary and sentence structure, they won't be able to do so.

DISSERTATION
CREATING A BIBLIOGRAPHY

THE BIBLIOGRAPHY

In your dissertation, and indeed in any academic writing, you will be expected to not only demonstrate knowledge of the topic you have chosen, but an ability to acquire 'an awareness of contexts – literary, historical, cultural, ideological' and to deploy 'evidence from secondary sources' (SQA).

This implies that you will be reading the works of other authors. As already highlighted, these are your sources or, when you are quoting from them, your references. At the end of your dissertation, you are expected to write a list of all the sources, primary and secondary, that you have read or referred to. You must provide clear details of the book title, the date of publication, who published it and where. This is your bibliography.

Why is it important to write down your references correctly?

Firstly, your examiners will be able to see evidence that you have read 'around' or researched your topic. They will also be able to see what type of books, articles and so on, that you've been reading, and that you have not just used the internet.

Secondly, if you don't reference your sources, you could be guilty of plagiarism – which, as was highlighted earlier, is very easy to do.

Finally, by including all the details of your sources, your examiners will be able – if they want – to go and look up a particular quote, or read more about a critic's point of view.

A quick guide to writing a bibliography

- A bibliography should be presented on a separate page with the title 'Bibliography'.
- All items should be included in alphabetical order by the surname of the author.
- All entries should be made in line with the following formats:
    - **Book – Single Author**

Aird, E. (1973) *Sylvia Plath*, Edinburgh, Oliver and Boyd

    - **Book – More than one author**

Calder, A., Calder, J., (1969) *Scott: Literature in Perspective*, London, Evans Brothers

    - **Edited Text**

Ridley, M. R. ed. (1968) Dr Jekyll and Mr Hyde, The Merry Men and Other Tales, London, Dent

    - **A poem**

Hughes, T., 'Hawk Roosting' in Hughes, T., (1960) *Lupercal*, London, Faber and Faber

    - **A play**

Williams, T., 'Cat on a Hot Tin Roof' in Williams, T., (1988) *Cat on a Hot Tin Roof and Other Plays*, Great Britain, Penguin

    - **Article**

MacGillvary, A., (2010) 'Natural Loyalties: The Work of William McIlvanney' in *The Association of Scottish Literary Studies*, Vol pp NB: If the volume and the pages are not available because the article has been accessed from a website, follow the instructions for this on p. 39.

    - **Newspaper Article**

The following can be used depending on the amount of information available:

The Independent, 25 March 2011

contd

Dissertation: Creating a bibliography

Taylor, P., 'Tennessee Williams: A tormented playwright who unzipped his heart' The Independent, 25 March 2011

- o **Reference Material (dictionaries, encyclopaedias)**

CHAMBERS TWENTIETH CENTURY DICTIONARY, ED BY A. M. Macdonald, Chambers, 1972

NEW ENCYCLOPAEDIA BRITANNICA. 15TH ED 32 VOLS. Encyclopaedia Britannica, 1986

Online material and websites

Including information which you have referenced from online can be quite daunting. The easiest way to do this is, if the online material or website has an author or title, it should be included in your bibliography in the same way as you would with any other type of material. But you must indicate that you are referencing online material or a website. You can do this simply by including the website address and, if possible, the date you accessed it.

Here's an example:

Seigle, L. Blanche Dubois: An Antihero www.bu.edu/writingprogram/journal/past-issues/issue-2/seigle/ Accessed 2 September 2017

If, as often happens, your online website has no author, just include it in alphabetical order of title in your bibliography.

Footnotes

A footnote is used for a reference that you've used in the text. Although a footnote can be inserted beside the actual words quoted or referred to, usually they are placed at the end of the relevant sentence, and, if possible, after a full stop. When entering a footnote, use the same format that you've used in your bibliography.

Including a footnote in the 'olden days' was a laborious and time-consuming task. Now, it can be done at the click of a button – and most word processors automatically number them for you. However, it's important that you do not litter your dissertation with them – use them correctly and they will add to the academic 'feel' of your dissertation.

 **DON'T FORGET**

This will be the last thing you will check. Whatever happens, be consistent and make sure that you don't include any author or reference that you've not quoted into your dissertation just to impress your examiner.

 THINGS TO DO AND THINK ABOUT

... and finally

You have now finished the last stage of the process – you have reached your destination.

You now know:

- what a dissertation is
- how to research a topic of your own choice
- how to use primary and secondary sources to help you form your own opinions
- how to take notes so that you can use them effectively
- how to plan and structure a long piece of writing
- how to write in a formal academic style
- how to present footnotes and a bibliography.

Initially, you were daunted by the prospect ahead of you. Now, you are at a point where you can communicate your ideas clearly and you are in complete control of your writing.

PORTFOLIO

APPROACHING PORTFOLIO WRITING

In case you were about to skip this chapter, *don't!* Yes, yes, we know you did well in portfolio writing in National 5 and Higher. Otherwise, you probably wouldn't be taking this course. But Advanced Higher English is your very last opportunity in school to fine-tune your writing skills.

You now need to consider the expectations of examiners in even greater depth. How well will your content, structure, tone, mood and expression *truly* stand up to intense scrutiny at the very highest level? How well in the past have you *really* got under the skin of your chosen genres?

When approaching these portfolio pieces, beware the danger of thinking 'I've done this all before'. You haven't. Yes, you've produced successful pieces for National 5 and Higher, but now the stakes have been raised. The best portfolio pieces at Advanced Higher English should be flirting with the level of competence and invention found in published articles and short stories. Are you prepared to say that you've brought your proficiency up to this standard yet?

Top marks at Advanced Higher English are certainly achievable, provided you're prepared to put in the necessary hard work. The portfolio you are about to present has to see you pushing your skills to ever-extended boundaries. Aim for these. You may well surprise yourself. And we're here to help you do just that!

WHAT ARE YOU BEING ASKED TO DO HERE?

Your writing pieces can be chosen from any two of the following genres:

- Persuasive
- Informative
- Poetry
- Drama
- Argumentative
- Reflective
- Prose fiction

Happily, you are free to choose any two genres you like; there is no obligation to write one discursive piece and one creative piece. As long as you write in two different genres, the choice is all yours.

Each piece should be at least 1000 words, with the exception of poetry which can be less. Each piece is worth up to 15 marks. Together, the portfolio pieces account for 30% of your final grade.

HOW CAN YOU ENHANCE YOUR WRITING?

Perhaps you haven't noticed, but since you first started writing folio pieces, you have been steadily maturing as a person; your writing skills have undergone a similar development. That's why you should abandon any thought of 'recycling' previous folio contributions. Examiners have a sixth sense for this and you would be doing yourself and your increased abilities a great disservice. Continued practice has made you a good writer. Now you need to be an even better one. Let's look at how you might achieve this.

Re-examine purpose and audience

Your purpose is to pass the exam with the best possible grade; your audience is the examining body. Correct? Well, only partly. This is the explicit purpose and audience; but consider, too, the implicit purpose and audience. In other words, how well does your piece stand

contd

up to real world scrutiny? Would a general reader of prose fiction be intrigued or moved by your short story and read it to the end? If your persuasive piece appeared in a newspaper or magazine, how seriously would your opinion and language be taken? At this late stage in your English studies, these are the questions you must ask yourself as you write.

Read for techniques

Writing well, as your English teachers have been telling you for years, requires you to read widely and often. But as exam pressures mount, this becomes increasingly difficult. At Advanced Higher English level, it could be productive to examine closely localised techniques practised by masters of your chosen genres.

Put specific examples of their writing under your microscope. In prose fiction, for example, look at how a professional writer may handle an opening paragraph. Look closely at sentence lengths, the detail of setting offered in the first lines, the first words a character utters. Are there any techniques here you could transfer to your own writing? In a persuasive newspaper article, how did the writer hook their readers; how did they lead in to another aspect of the topic; how did they round it off? What could you take away from here?

ONLINE

Head to www.brightredbooks.net for links to great examples of travel writing.

Such an approach does not necessitate spending hours reading the complete works of specific writers, but a forensic examination of the *detail* of well-crafted writing can pay valuable dividends.

How the best of the internet can help

If you are considering prose fiction, drama or poetry, your school library is still the best place to start your forensic examination of successful techniques. If you're attracted by persuasive, reflective, informative or argumentative writing, the internet is a valuable mine of texts for study.

One area where the techniques for both creative and discursive writing can sometimes come together is in travel writing. Travel writers are a curious mixture of the creative and analytical. The best of them have much to offer the apprentice writer.

Follow the links on the Digital Zone for travel articles for some varied and imaginative approaches to the genre. Read for enjoyment, of course, but at the same time read to pick up tips and strategies to enrich the writing and reading experience.

ONLINE

Would-be discursive writer? For a broad selection of award-winning articles, visit www.brightredbooks.net Not only do the examples there offer insights into techniques, but they often throw up issues of the day, with recently researched information for persuasive, argumentative and informative work.

THINGS TO DO AND THINK ABOUT

A good portfolio takes time, and this is where this study guide can help. Go through the various, more popular genres analysed here. How well do they sit with your writing abilities? Think carefully about the genres in which you feel comfortable, or genres in which you may have already had some success. List possibilities and consider fully their specific requirements before making any decision. Leave plenty of time, too, for researching, drafting, re-drafting and final editing. Today might be a good time to start!

DON'T FORGET

The ability to write well is one of the factors which differentiates high-flyers from the rest. And not just at school ... it's a skill for life.

PORTFOLIO

PROSE FICTION (PART 1)

At this level, there are numerous formats your creative writing can follow. You may, of course, wish to continue to develop your skills in short-story writing, or pursue creating the opening, conclusion or a key episode from a novel. But other possibilities worthy of consideration are:

- a focused piece of characterisation
- a monologue or dialogue
- a detailed description of an imaginary setting
- a series of diary entries
- an exchange of letters.

While the choices are varied, many share common features such as:

- a plot or narrative framework built around credible characters whose evolving situation leads to some kind of denouement
- a recognisable structure which holds together the narrative
- thoughtful use of dialogue, imagery and symbolism
- an authorial stance or tone, not necessarily intrusive or obvious, which reveals the writer's ability to shape the material.

To offer your audience a rich reading experience, you need to be alert to the possibilities these factors can bring to a text and manipulate them appropriately.

THREE USEFUL PILLARS

In a number of prose fiction formats, the foundation of a rich reading experience is based on characterisation, setting and plot.

Characterisation: the importance of detail

Here is award-winning novelist Colm Tóibín 'hooking' his readers in an opening which might usefully be examined by anyone trying to establish characterisation in a short story, an episode from a novel or a focused piece of characterisation:

> *Eilis Lacey, sitting at the window of the upstairs living room in the house in Friary Street, noticed her sister walking briskly from work. She watched Rose crossing the street from sunlight into shade, carrying the new leather handbag that she had bought in Clery's in Dublin in the sale. Rose was wearing a cream-coloured cardigan over her shoulders. Her golf-clubs were in the hall; in a few minutes, Eilis knew, someone would call for her and her sister would not return until the summer evening had faded.*

Tóibín, C, (2015) *Brooklyn*, London, Penguin, p. 3

There is little here that does not, with great economy, immediately situate the two women in the reader's mind.

TEXTUAL DETAIL	WHAT THE WRITER SUGGESTS
'Eilis Lacey, sitting at the window'	At the story's opening, Eilis is the quiet observer of her more active sister, Rose. Will this always be the case?
'crossing the street from sunlight into shade'	Might this be suggesting a later change in Rose's fortunes?
'walking briskly from work'	Even after her day's work, Rose retains an energetic purposefulness.
'the new leather handbag she had bought […] in the sale'	Rose may be fashion-conscious but she is also money-conscious.
'someone would call for her […] would not return until the summer evening had faded'	Rose is popular and socially active.

contd

Although perhaps we learn more here about Rose than Eilis, both sisters are brought alive by Tóibín's concern with **detail**, and the detail is working hard to establish both the circusmstances and key characteristics of both girls which will be developed later. Ensure your characters are amply detailed, and that the detail is there **for a purpose**. Make sure the detail you introduce can help you develop the character later, otherwise you are word-spinning to no real end.

Characterisation: methods of creation

Characterisation can be made to come alive for readers in a variety of ways. As you write, be constantly alert to various methods at your disposal for creating convincing characters. For a list of some of them, look at page 69 in the characterisation section of the *Textual Analysis* chapter.

By now, you are well accustomed to analysing characters in fiction for critical comment. Now it's your turn to write, make your accumulated knowledge in this sphere work for you! For additional suggestions see pages 98–99 in Bright Red's *Study Guide for Higher English*.

Setting: beyond a sense of place

Deft manipulation of setting is an important factor in successful creative writing, whatever the format. Just as successful character creation is grounded in detail, so, too, is setting. The opening of George Orwell's *1984* situates his hero in a physical setting that gives an insight into his environment and hints at his emotional state – both features to be developed later in the text:

> *It was a bright cold day in April, and the clocks were striking thirteen. Winston Smith, his chin nuzzled into his breast in an effort to escape the vile wind, slipped quickly through the glass doors of Victory Mansions, though not quickly enough to prevent a swirl of gritty dust from entering along with him. The hallway smelt of boiled cabbage and old rag mats.*

Orwell, G. (2004) *1984*, London, Penguin, p. 3

TEXTUAL DETAIL	WHAT THE WRITER SUGGESTS
'a bright cold day in April'	First words might suggest a typical spring day …
'the clocks were striking thirteen.'	… but suddenly normality is thrown into confusion. Clocks do not strike thirteen in a normal world.
'his chin nuzzled into his breast'	Hero seeking comfort and shelter from the 'vile' wind. But maybe from more than that?
'Victory Mansions'	Proud sounding. But whose victory?
'a swirl of gritty dust'	Unpleasantness felt through the sense of touch.
'smelt of boiled cabbage and old rag mats'	Unpleasantness felt through sense of smell.

Orwell, through subtle detailing in the opening setting, suggests a world which, on the surface, appears loosely normal, yet, examined more closely, comes across as bleakly unpleasant. Given this oppressive opening setting, we are not unduly surprised when the novel goes on to explore the evils of a fascist state.

 THINGS TO DO AND THINK ABOUT

Look back at Tóibín's opening to *Brooklyn*. Notice that, although Eilis picks out only a few details of Rose's appearance, she captures the essence of the woman (as we learn when we read on).

In a few lines, experiment with a similar approach to establishing a character with just a few details. Use this 'observer-at-a-window' technique on a person you already know quite well. Try to make your use of detail **purposeful**, not merely descriptive. In other words, could these details be developed later in a full-scale practice piece?

DON'T FORGET

Characterisation can be enhanced by your characters' ways of conversing. Be alert to the usefulness of dialect. Bossiness, insecurity, vagueness and so on can all emerge in the sentence structure of dialogue, helping to differentiate characters.

 ONLINE

Head to www.brightredbooks.net to read the article 'Evoke a sense of place' by Judy Darley. She is a keen observer of the power of setting in fiction.

PORTFOLIO

PROSE FICTION (PART 2)

SETTING: A LEVER FOR CHANGE

Settings, like people, can change. Changes in place, time, season and weather can mirror the fortunes and moods of your characters. Altering the setting in the course of your narrative can do much to move on the action. Let's see how that might work:

TIME OF DAY	Times of day, like words, have connotations. Morning, in narratives, is often associated with new beginnings and fresh hope; evening may suggest the end of something; and night can be threatening.
SEASON	Seasons, too, carry connotations with them: spring – hope; summer – ripeness and harvest; autumn – the hint of an ending; winter – cold and death of the year. You could, of course, turn these connotations completely on their head to create contrasts, for example, sadness in spring when everything else feels full of life. A change of season could signal a key change in your narrative.
WEATHER	Weather is a powerful way of supporting the atmosphere you are creating around your characters. For instance, when something is starting to go wrong in a good relationship, maybe there is a rumble of distant summer thunder. Think how film directors use weather changes to alter the mood of scenarios.
OBJECTS	Something simple like a vase of flowers can add greatly to your story-telling. Fresh flowers; a few petals scattered on a table top; withered blooms in a dry vase – all these can signal landmark moments in an evolving narrative.

DON'T FORGET

Changes in setting can help you to underline both the changing mood of your narrative or the altered state of your characters' fortunes.

PLOTTING

The plot in prose fiction at Advanced Higher level does not need to be complicated, but it does need to be controlled. This means that your cast list cannot be too extensive, nor the time scale too ambitious. Plot should be a flexible framework, within which theme(s), characters and settings have scope to emerge naturally.

There are endless structural possibilities here. If you're at a loss for a structure, the following one has proved useful on many occasions:

- A settled situation involving a minimum of characters (perhaps two or three).

- A complication deriving from something happening: a letter arriving, an accident, a serious illness, a new character appearing, the loss of someone or something.

- An increase in tension due to the new situation.

- A crisis leading to a turning point in the affairs of all concerned.

- An ending with a perceived change in matters compared with how they stood at the start. Perhaps the unhappy are now happier; perhaps a relationship has altered, for better or for worse; perhaps characters have simply changed their view of themselves or someone else; or perhaps we readers have changed our perception of a character or situation.

You can probably think of many narratives which use only some of these features or perhaps none at all. Don't be tied down by this suggestion, but it may help you get started.

IMAGERY AND SYMBOLISM

No matter the format your prose fiction may take, imagery and symbolism are vital to enriching both the texture of your writing and the reading experience of your audience.

Imagery such as metaphors, similes, personification, etc. are familiar to you from years of textual analysis and RUAE. But don't overlook their usefulness when it comes to your own writing. Characters and setting alike benefit from added depth when imagery fleshes out their outlines.

contd

In the relatively short writing pieces you're being asked to produce here, symbolism (which is only a form of imagery itself) can be a handy economical way of saying quite a lot. It's simply a way of using an object, person, colour or situation to represent or suggest something else. Symbols can turn up in various guises.

Colour

- Green can be seen as a symbol of new hope, growth, or as ecologically friendly. But it can also be associated with envy.
- White is usually the universal symbol of purity and innocence.
- Black is often seen as representing something negative or downright evil.
- Red is often associated with passion or danger.
- Blue may be seen as connected with calm, cold or iciness.

These associations are a useful shorthand for writers as their connotations are generally understood. So, the colours of your characters' clothes, cars, etc. can be employed to make points about their life choices.

Objects

These can act as a kind of concretised metaphor for the themes at which you may be hinting. Among the more common you may find the following:

- Locks, bars, safes – to suggest a desire to keep people out or secrets in (as in *The Strange Case of Dr Jekyll and Mr Hyde*).
- Birds and their flight – to symbolise release and freedom. Caged birds can suggest much about their owners ... victims or jailers?
- Fires – to suggest a strong life force (an empty hearth its opposite), or people of strong passion, perhaps bordering on the dangerous.
- Water – to suggest fertility and growth; or, conversely, drought, sterility or death.
- Glass and glass objects – to symbolise fragility or transparency of personality.

Used sparingly, objects can make telling points about characters and themes. They should be used often enough to be noticed, but not too often to become repetitively tiresome.

Motifs

A motif is an idea or concept (rather than an object) that repeats throughout the narrative, in a way which subtly infiltrates the reader's consciousness. Used well, a motif is never obtrusive but helps to create a cohesive effect, aiding the establishment of a theme. Here are some examples:

- Loss: this idea may occur in various forms – the death of a friend; fading memory; homesickness; loss of physical powers.
- Oppression: in a narrative this may appear at a national, social and familial level.
- Darkness: this may be quite literal, or signal moral corruption.
- Vision: clear-sightedness suggests idealism or hope for the future; short-sightedness, or loss of sight, could be seen as moral blindness.

Sparingly used, such elements can help establish your theme(s). But, remember, like other forms of symbolism, overuse can be intrusive.

 **DON'T FORGET**

Symbolism is a useful shorthand for establishing character, setting and theme(s). Employed thoughtfully, it will add a professional gloss to your writing.

 ONLINE

For a useful insight into the usefulness of symbolism, read '5 Important Ways to Use Symbolism in Your Story' on the Digital Zone.

 THINGS TO DO AND THINK ABOUT

Symbols do not have to be universal. Anything can be a symbol in your narrative, provided it has meaning for the characters involved – for example, a teddy bear, a garden, or a piece of music. In an evolving relationship, these can be employed to symbolise various stages such as cherished, neglected, or abandoned.

PORTFOLIO
REFLECTIVE

Many students find a reflective essay the most rewarding portfolio task of all. For here is a chance to get down on paper certain thoughts which may have been with you for some time. Not only is it a chance to examine the ideas in depth, but it's also a chance to explore your own identity in response to these thoughts.

You will be assessed on your insights into your chosen topic, but also on your success in communicating to readers a real sense of your own personality.

AREAS FOR REFLECTION

Your life experience is already rich in possible topics for scrutiny. The possibilities are almost limitless, but to jog your memory here are a few ideas:

- A person; a place; an object
- A condition; a situation; a feeling
- An image; an idea; an insight
- An issue; an activity; a theory; a belief

What are you aiming for?

Your aim here, as in all your portfolio work, is to provide readers with as rewarding a reading experience as possible. This means drawing on all the writing techniques you have at your disposal, just as you would in prose fiction. The main difference is that your raw material is anchored in reality rather than imagination. Your purpose is to interest your readers by sharing your insights with them in an engaging manner. By the end of your essay, they should have a comprehensive view of you as a thinker, writer and human being.

How do you go about this?

CHARACTER PRESENTATION	You are at the heart of this essay, so use the 'I' pronoun unapologetically.
	While remaining natural, you should think about how you present this 'I'. If people are to be interested in – and perhaps convinced by – your reflections, you need to present yourself as someone who thinks in a balanced way, and who is aware of and open to the ideas and reactions of others. Indeed, the views of others may have been a factor in making up your own mind on the topic ... 'Now, take my English teacher. Unlike me, she finds ...'
LANGUAGE CHOICES	Your language choices will colour the personality that emerges. It's always more attractive to talk *to* rather than *at* the reader.
	Informal tone is key to striking the right note in an essay of this kind because it suggests that you're exchanging views with a friend. (In case you need reminding of the key features of informal tone, see pages 22–23 of Bright Red's *Higher English Study Guide*. But be careful not to overuse the rhetorical question!)
	In confiding your views to your readers, do not overlook opportunities to enrich your text with imagery. Metaphors and similes are as illuminating here as in prose fiction.

contd

Portfolio: Reflective

EXPLORING PROCESS	Your stance is contemplative; your tone confiding. In fact, if you can persuade your readers that they are overhearing you as you explore your topic – letting them in on the process of a mind making itself up, as it were – you are close to the essence of fine reflective writing.
	In the process, you may work through several moods: intrigued/interested by the topic itself; indignant at times perhaps because this topic seems to be misunderstood; concerned by the possible effects of this misunderstanding; and amused at times by the superficiality of critics.
	The process of arriving at your conclusion is as important as the conclusion itself. Signal changes of mood and tone clearly to ensure your essay maintains an overall structural unity.
INTRODUCTORY MOVES	Sharing with your readers how your interest in the topic first came about is one useful way to 'hook' them. (But be careful that this anecdote does not take over the essay.)
	It's also sensible to make clear why you believe the topic is worthy of attention, offering any background information you think necessary.
	Just as the opening of a piece of prose fiction should draw people in immediately, so, too, should the opening remarks of a reflective essay.

 DON'T FORGET

Make sure you choose a subject for a reflective essay which has adequate depth to be mulled over from various angles.

 DON'T FORGET

Humour in a reflective essay can make a serious point as effectively as factual information.

 THINGS TO DO AND THINK ABOUT

Choosing the right topic for a reflective essay can take time. With a partner, brainstorm some of the issues/topics/activities which intrigue, concern, amuse or irritate you. List them and decide which ones might offer sufficient depth and angles to sustain your own interest and that of your reader.

Once you have a 'front-runner', list the angles and viewpoints from which you might approach this topic.

PORTFOLIO
PERSUASIVE

This is a favourite among those of you who have strong convictions on aspects of the world around us. In a persuasive essay, you aim to persuade readers to adopt your viewpoint. To do this successfully, you will need to manipulate language – quite shamelessly – to work on your readers at both an intellectual and emotional level.

CHOOSING THE RIGHT LANGUAGE

You're far from being a neutral commentator on your subject; you are wholly committed to changing perceptions. Luckily, you have many language choices to help you get your readers onside. Here are some to think about:

Make yourself a friend	Be generous with use of 'you', 'we' and 'us'. (We're friends after all, aren't we?) *We're all surely alike in thinking that … You, like me, may well feel … every time we see …*
Chat them up	Conversational tone is a sound way to get close to readers. Informality can be established with abbreviations such as 'it's', 'we're', 'couldn't'; and, from time to time, use short/minor sentences for effect: *'And no wonder!'* (Check out more examples of informal tone on pages 22–23 of Bright Red's *Higher English Study Guide*.)
Use informal commands	You're not being bossy here, just inviting readers to join you in a flight of fancy. *Imagine a world in which children no longer … Just think how much better life would be for us all if …*
Employ emotive terms	Take every opportunity to work on readers' feelings by making your vocabulary work hard at an emotional level. Load descriptions with emotive adjectives and adverbs: *pitiful medical supplies, grossly undernourished refugees, seriously over-worked nursing staff …* You want here to arouse sympathy for victims and anger at those responsible for their plight.
Celebrate your heroes	If you cite the action or speeches of someone well known and supportive of your viewpoint, load their name with a phrase in apposition: *Charles Dickens, that great champion of the poor, was surely right when he said …* *Al Gore, a brave defender of our planet, maintains that …*
Ask rhetorical questions	These are questions which expect no real answer; their real purpose is to elicit the reader's approval and support: *Who would have thought it would come to this? Is this the kind of education we want for our children?* Note, however, that some in public life take it on themselves to answer these very questions that expect no answer! *No, it's far from being the education we want for our children! And I'll tell you why! What we want is …* This might be a technique to use in places. But beware of too many rhetorical questions; used too often, they begin to sound a bit hollow and could make you come across as a real old wind-bag!
Drop in attitude markers	With these single words at the beginning of sentences, you are nudging readers to adopt a certain attitude towards a point of view. Yours! *Surely … Obviously … Clearly … Undoubtedly …*

contd

Think in threes!	Politicians and advertisers long ago discovered that you can make a great emotional appeal by presenting your ideas in threes. These 'threes' may take several forms.
	Repetition – Sometimes a powerful effect can be made by simply repeating a single word: We <u>cannot</u> accept her claim that ... We <u>cannot</u> allow her to ... We <u>cannot</u> support her when she ...
	Parallel structures – Recurring patterns in phrases are a memorable way to present a persuasive message: <u>We welcome the frankness</u> of her demand that ... <u>We admire the honesty</u> of her confession that ... <u>We share the generosity</u> of her vision which foresees ...
	Tricolons (or rising rhetorical triads) – These are often favoured towards the end of rousing speeches and work well at the close of persuasive essays, too. Each sentence, by taking phrases repeated from earlier statements, seeks to build in power towards one ringing final statement: <u>Let us hope these moves will</u> begin to ... <u>Let us hope they will also</u> bring about a situation in which ... <u>But let us hope most of all that</u>, finally, we shall all be able to say ...

The need for sound content

In your desire to change reader perceptions, do not let concerns of style overtake the necessity for sound factual content. Your case must be based on information as up-to-date and as carefully researched as the material in a more sober argumentative or informative essay. People can be persuaded, but they cannot be fooled, especially by material that is patently thin. If it is a 'hot' topic of the moment, see what leading thinkers are suggesting by examining online quality newspapers. Style is important, but so is content.

STRUCTURING YOUR MATERIAL

To win over your readers, it's wise to present yourself as a sensible, reasonable character. And sensible, reasonable characters are always aware that other people may have opposing views. How do we deal with them? Just ignore them? That could make you appear ignorant and unaware of the world around you. Your structure needs to consider how best to deal with these contrary views and build in a way of defusing them. Here is a possible structural framework:

- An introduction in which you lay out the topic's importance and significance. Then you quickly make your viewpoint clear.
- You acknowledge that a conflicting view may exist, but you refute it in a reasonable, but **brief**, way. Avoid being aggressive or offensive in your rejection.
- Launch your first persuasive paragraph.
- Continue with similarly persuasive paragraphs, **saving your strongest argument until last**.
- A conclusion in which you draw together again your main arguments from the body of the essay, ending perhaps with some stirring use of tricolons (rising rhetorical triads).

 **DON'T FORGET**

Research suggests that people remember best the last thing they have been told. So save your best argument to the end!

 ONLINE

For some good examples of persuasive writing, follow the link to the 'debatabase' at www.brightredbooks.net

 THINGS TO DO AND THINK ABOUT

If writing a persuasive piece appeals to you, get in a little practice right now. Visit the 'debatabase' online and read a few of the debates on culture, economy, education, environment, etc.

Examine the points for and against a topic that interests you. Using as many persuasive devices as seem sensible, work up a suitably persuasive introduction. Read it to a partner. Get feedback on style and content. Does the topic appeal sufficiently to be the basis for a folio piece?

PORTFOLIO
POETRY

From your textual analysis work for this and previous courses, you know that defining the essence of poetry is a challenging task. You are not alone in finding it so. Libraries of books have been written on the subject, and few of them agree with each other. Therefore, writing a poem of your own – one with real creative integrity – ratchets up the challenge a good few notches.

WHAT ARE YOU BEING ASKED TO DO?

Although you may write fewer words here than in other folio pieces, the poetry option is by no means an easier option. The assessment criteria are just as demanding.

Content should demonstrate depth and complexity of reflection. You should be able to develop this reflection throughout the poem's structure. Think of the poems you are studying in your *Textual Analysis* work; they offer the depth of thought for which you should be aiming here. This is no easy exercise in superficial rhyming!

Structure is a key element in this project. Whether you opt for a traditional poetic form or for a poem in free verse, how your poem is held together will be closely examined. In a traditional format, structure is fairly easily identifiable, but in free verse you need to think of a less obvious, but equally rigorous, network of cohesive techniques. Structural organisation, whether obvious or discreet, is necessary if your writing is to have the required impact.

Expression, while important in all your writing, is perhaps even more keenly prized here. For poetry, by its very nature, has to demonstrate both a heightened awareness of connotations and originality in image making. Sensitivity, too, to the patterning of the rhythm and sound of words is equally vital.

In the *Textual Analysis* chapter of this guide, you will find guidance on the resources that poets regularly draw upon to create their work. Checking out all of the possiblities before you start to write would be time well spent.

ONLINE

You'll find a link to the Scottish Poetry Library's website at www.brightredbooks.net Select the 'POETRY read and explore' section; then tap the 'Browse by tag' button. These tags offer a huge choice of poems written on a variety of topics.

WHAT SHOULD YOU WRITE ABOUT?

When posed with this question, professional writers would suggest you write about what you know best – you and your life experience. Topics that you are considering for a reflective essay might also provide useful raw materials for a poem. Powerful poems require a ring of conviction about them – and this is most surely conveyed when you really know what you are talking about.

Detail is also important in illuminating these experiences; no one was ever moved by generalisations. Think about how sensitive word choice, figurative language, rhythm, rhyme, alliteration, assonance, onomatopoeia, and all the other poetic devices you have studied, can be harnessed to bring alive the central idea(s) of your own poem.

IN WHAT FORM MIGHT YOU WRITE?

Your poetry studies to date have probably taken you through a number of traditional forms: the sonnet, ballad, haiku, dramatic monologue, elegy, ode, etc. There is insufficient space in a guide of this kind to explore all the forms you might choose. But this is a moment to look at the *Textual Analysis* chapter of this guide for a detailed analysis of how a sonnet (Shakespeare pages 60–61) or a poem in free verse (Alan Riach page 67) might be structured. Here you will see how content and form come together to create a successful unity to offer the reader. How might **your** content and form merge?

contd

Portfolio: Poetry

What resources might help?

As was suggested earlier, your own life experience might be a useful platform for your writing. But it is always valuable to see how others have turned their life experience into poetry. From your N5 and Higher studies, you may have already seen how poets like Jackie Kay, Norman MacCaig, Edwin Morgan and Liz Lochhead have approached examining their personal responses to life situations. It would also be worth exploring the resources of the Scottish Poetry Library.

Below are a few tags which may touch your own experience, and a few particular poems that might be useful to study more closely. But these are just a few of hundreds at your disposal!

TAG	A FEW SUGGESTED POEM(S)
Identity	'Same, Difference' by Robert Crawford; 'just another pebble' by Eunice Buchanan
Writing poetry	'Bad Moon' by Claire Askew; 'Seven Decades' by Edwin Morgan
Families	'Old Photograph' by Hugh McMillan
Man and nature	'Field-Mouse's Nest' by John Clare; 'North of Berwick' by Sydney Tremayne
Nature	'Autumn at Kincraig' by Tessa Ransford; 'The Ash Grove' by Ken Cockburn

VIDEO LINK

Watch a recitation of Fanthorpe's 'Not My Best Side' at www.brightredbooks.net to see how the poet manipulates language to great effect.

Look carefully at the structuring devices these poets have employed to shape their ideas. Could any of these be of use to you as as a framework?

Capturing a voice

Many poems draw their success from capturing a voice or tone of voice. The poet U. A. Fanthorpe takes a well-known painting, *Saint George and the Dragon* by Paolo Uccello, and gives each of the three figures illustrated – the dragon, the knight and the damsel in distress – a very individual voice and personality in her poem 'Not my Best Side'. Each uses language very differently to comment on the same situation.

Could another work of art offer you a similar opportunity to talk in the personality and language of one or more of the characters depicted?

Uccello, P. *Saint George and the Dragon*, Oil on canvas. National Gallery, London.

 ## THINGS TO DO AND THINK ABOUT

If you're not sure whether to employ a traditional form or free verse for your ideas once you have formulated them in draft form, try writing a few opening lines in both formats. Although this is still only a rough draft, ask someone whose judgement you value for their opinion as to which carries most conviction. The final choice has to be yours, but a second or even third opinion can be helpful at this stage.

 ### DON'T FORGET

As you write, keep asking yourself if you are as sensitive to the sound and rhythm of your words as to the sense of them. The 'music' of your words will greatly enhance the communication of your ideas.

PORTFOLIO

DRAMA

A drama piece for your portfolio may take many forms. You have the choice of a one-act play, an opening scene of a play, a dramatic monologue, a radio play, a television sitcom, a storyboard, shooting script, a film script or a documentary drama. While the breadth of the dramatic challenges on offer may appear vastly different from the challenges of prose fiction, the two genres share a similar insistence on sympathetic characters, convincing settings and a plausible plot. How then are these to be realised in the context of a drama?

CHARACTERS

While personality can be fully established with descriptive paragraphs in prose fiction, your onstage characters depend entirely on their appearance, their speech, their actions and their movement to come across as credible people to your audience. Capturing a fully rounded character depends on being constantly alert to the implications of all these aspects of your creations.

Show, don't tell

In this briefest of extracts, the speech, actions and movements on display tell us a great deal about the three main characters and their relationship to each other.

> *TOM: I haven't enjoyed one bite of this dinner because of your constant directions on how to eat it. It's you that makes me rush through meals with your hawk-like attention to every bite I take. Sickening – spoils my appetite – all this discussion of animals' secretion ... salivary glands ... mastication!*
>
> *AMANDA [lightly]: Temperament like a Metropolitan star! [He rises and crosses downstage.] You're not excused from the table.*
>
> *TOM: I'm getting a cigarette.*
>
> *AMANDA: You smoke too much.*
>
> *[LAURA rises.]*
>
> *LAURA: I'll bring in the blancmangé. [He remains standing with his cigarette by the portières during the following.]*

Williams, T. (2009) *The Glass Menagerie*, Scene 1, Penguin Modern Classics, London, p. 6

The rebelliousness of Tom; the controlling streak of his mother, Amanda; and the desire to avoid confrontation by Laura are all deftly sketched in, preparing the audience for the direction the later action may take. You need to be equally alert to establishing your characters and their relationships with each other by such **economical** interaction and dialogue.

contd

Character considerations

When creating your characters, it might be useful to keep in mind the following:

KNOW THEM – To know your characters thoroughly, it might be helpful to construct a table of biographic details for your own use. If your characters are not fully alive to you, you cannot expect your audience to believe in them.	**LIMIT THEM** – If you are to characterise fully your cast, it might be best to limit their number so that you can bring each one alive with distinctive personalities.
CONTRAST THEM – One of the best sources of drama in any situation is frequently the confrontation of conflicting personalities and viewpoints. Conflict between your characters will keep your script moving briskly forward.	**DEVELOP THEM** – Consider how the action of the script will have an impact on the lives of your characters. How will they change or be changed? But such change needs to be managed gradually, by credible actions or happenings.

Sourcing characters

Professional writers are quick to tell you that you write best about what you know best. Certain behavioural characteristics of your friends and family might furnish distinctive aspects of your characters. Think, too, of all the texts you've been reading over the last few years. By adapting character traits from familiar characters in prose fiction, poetry and drama, you might end up with a convincing character of your own.

By examining the private life of two minor characters in *Hamlet,* the playwright Tom Stoppard created one of his most successful plays – *Rosencrantz and Guildenstern are Dead*. Reflect on any plays you studied for Higher English. Are there any minor characters there whose private lives might bear a closer look?

Avoid characters sounding the same

A good dramatic text is not primarily about words on a page; it is about the living voice. The way people speak differentiates them as much as their looks, hair and eye colour. In fact, you could argue that the way people speak is perhaps the clearest guide to their core personality. In a dramatic monologue such as *Shirley Valentine* or one of Alan Bennett's *Talking Heads* series, it is the speaker's speech patterns that ultimately define individual personalities.

Consider, too, Lynne Truss's *A Certain Age* series for useful tips on language-driven character creation. Sentence length, sentence structures, slang and favoured phrases all contribute to the final individual profile. Bossiness, insecurity, dynamism and vagueness are expressed not only by **what** characters say but **how** they express themselves. Make sure you build appropriate speech patterns into your final creation. Contrasting speech patterns, as well as contrasting characters, will help determine the audience's response to your cast.

Consider subtext

As well as thinking about what characters say and how they say it, think, too, about what is not said overtly. In other words, the subtext. This may take the form of characters talking about one subject while their thoughts are on something else. These thoughts may ultimately be revealed and developed as part of the later action. A couple disagreeing about a film might give an insight into a failing relationship; an older person panicking about the loss of a document might suggest a larger concern about fading capacities. An alertness to the opportunities offered by subtextual elements will help enrich your script significantly.

> **DON'T FORGET**
>
> Successful dialogue benefits from shorter sentences than prose. And it doesn't always need to be delivered in fully formed sentences. Say it aloud as you write. Does it sound natural?

 THINGS TO DO AND THINK ABOUT

Find the clip of 'Miss Fozzard Finds her Feet' at www.brightredbooks.net, one of Alan Bennett's *Talking Heads*. Listen to how the playwright manipulates language for particular effects. While you may not be considering a monologue yourself, this is a master lesson in how to use speech characteristics to create character.

PORTFOLIO
PRACTICALITIES OF DRAMA

A fully realised setting is part of the dramatic experience. The more convincing the setting, the more convincing your script. Do not allow the personal circumstances of your characters to lead you to forget the contribution that their surroundings can make.

In *Macbeth*, Duncan's comments on his arrival at his host's residence are deeply ironic:

> This castle hath a pleasant seat; the air
> Nimbly and seetly recommmends itself
> Unto our gentle senses.

For it is in this pleasant-seeming castle that Duncan will meet his brutal death. Shakespeare has used the setting ironically, linking its deceiving appearance with the theme of false appearance elsewhere in the play.

Consider how your setting can contribute to the theme(s) you wish to express. Are your characters at variance in some way with their setting? Are they hostile to wealth? Frustrated by poverty? Angry with injustice? Or does their setting fully reflect their inner self?

Make the setting work

Make sure you give the setting a purpose to fulfil. A mountainside hints at danger – does your drama exploit this setting? How about a hospital waiting room? Is it leading us on to despair or hope? If you've taken the trouble to create a setting, use it.

Settings have their own language. For example, if the scene is taking place in the changing room of a gym, use the dialogue opportunities the place offers. Weave references to it into the dramatic narrative to create a credible situation rather than simply a meeting place for talking heads:

> FERGUS: It's as I was saying, we need to …
>
> CHRIS: Will you look at the state of this shower!
>
> FERGUS: … make sure we don't let him get away with anything like he did last time. He's more than likely to wriggle out of any responsibility for the disappearing money.
>
> CHRIS: Aaaagh! This water is freezing! What the hell do we pay £19.99 a month for? OK, OK, but that's easier said than done, my macho friend. But how exactly do you propose we do that?

Exploit stagecraft

Lighting, sound effects, costume changes and music all flesh out the words you have written in a way denied to the writer of prose fiction. Be alert to how a change of lighting can effectively emphasise a darkening or lightening mood. Think how a rumble of distant thunder might herald looming trouble. Consider how a change of costume might underline changed circumstances or mood. What might a violent character's fondness for listening unobserved to Beethoven's *Moonlight Sonata* suggest about his inner self? And what might a character's association with a prop such as a collection of glass animals suggest about her underlying personality?

As you write your script, do not become so engrossed in your text that you overlook the opportunities afforded by the multiple techniques of stagecraft. See the drama section of the *Textual Analysis* chapter of this book to review what you have at your disposal in this area.

PAGE LAYOUT

A script is potentially a performance document, so layout needs to be clear and uncluttered for the benefit of the actors.

- A separate title page giving both the title of the script and the author's name adds a certain professional touch to the presentation. This page could also carry the **dramatis personae** – that is, a list of the characters appearing in the scene and a brief description of their role, for example:

  Dr Percy: Elspeth's English teacher.

- The heading of the scene should carry the scene's title and briefly describe (in italics) the scene of the action, for example:

  NO HEAD FOR HEIGHTS
  A village high street in the Highlands. The present day.

- Names of characters should be in capital letters and set close in to the left of the page. (In some plays you will see names are followed by a colon.) Leave plenty of space between the name of the character and their lines, simply for ease of reading.

- For ease of reading, stage directions which occur outside a speech should be indented to line up with the actors' speeches. In this way, nothing interrupts the actors' line of vision as they scan the script for their lines. There is no need to use brackets here but italics will help separate them from the actors' lines.

- Stage directions which are linked to a certain speech should be in brackets. Putting them in italics avoids any confusion with the actors' lines.

CROFTER:	*(brightly)* Och aye!
	Doorbell rings.
WIFE:	Get your shoes on, that'll be the tourists from Rotherham, Yorks, and put some peat on top of that coal – they'll think we're no better than themselves.
CROFTER:	Aye, aye, aye – go you and let them in …
WIFE:	Put off that television and hunt for Jimmy Shand on the wireless.
	Crofter mimes this action.
	Oh God, there's the Marvel milk on the table, and I told them we had our own cows –

McGrath, J. (1974) *The Cheviot, the Stag and the Black, Black Oil*, London, Methuen Drama, p. 70

 **DON'T FORGET**

Music can help illustrate a situation, a setting, a mood or a personality. Changes in these can also be signalled by music. Check if, and how, your script would benefit from a musical soundtrack in places.

 ONLINE

For more on using songs in plays, follow the link on the Digital Zone. What this site has to say about 'Using Popular Songs' is well worth reading if you're thinking about introducing music to your script.

 ### THINGS TO DO AND THINK ABOUT

Consider settings you know well from your own experience. Choose one which you think helps reflect the society you live in. Experiment with a few lines of dialogue in which the setting comes alive for an audience. Could this be developed into a fully fledged scene?

PORTFOLIO

ARGUMENTATIVE

In a successful argumentative essay, writers take a topic over which there is some debate, and conduct in-depth research before presenting data to support both sides of the argument. Finally, if they so choose, they may award support to one viewpoint or the other.

Balance of factual presentation and neutrality of language are the hallmarks of this form of essay. Its tone is a far cry from the emotive one found in persuasive essays. Here, empirical facts and authority sourced from subject-specific experts and surveys colour the tone.

MAKING A START

As in your dissertation, the opening paragraph is particularly important for establishing your credentials as a reliable investigator of the topic. It needs to suggest you are:

- reliably informed
- articulate in presenting opposing viewpoints
- balanced in your assessment of them.

Articulating a title

The balanced nature of your arguments can be made clear in the title itself. 'Closed-Circuit Television: friend or foe?'; 'Health care: to pay or not to pay?'; 'The gap year: time wasted or an investment in the future?'

Since you will have researched your topic and may have arrived at a personal stance on it, it might be politic to award the final position in the title (for example, 'foe', 'not to pay' or 'investment in the future') to your own viewpoint (should you decide to support this stance). Why? Because it seems sensible to leave readers with your chosen viewpoint rather than opposing arguments – and the positioning of the title's wording prefigures this subtly. But we shall consider this prioritisation later in the section.

Organising your introduction

It's helpful for the reader if your introduction performs several tasks:

- To make clear the significance of the topic to our lives:

> *Last year in Britain, 20 000 lives were lost simply because ...*

- To provide brief background information which may be key to understanding the topic:

> *CCTV is surveillance by cameras to transmit an image to a central control which monitors security in places where security might be an issue. It was first installed in 1942 by ...*

- To set out the two opposing viewpoints which will be discussed:

> *For some, a gap year is seen as a total waste of time, time which might be better spent developing ... For others, it is time well spent, allowing as it does teenagers to discover the world and explore their personalities ...*

- To suggest a 'road-map' to the development of the essay:

contd

Portfolio: Argumentative

In seeking to determine the validity of each of these opposing stances, this study will look at the case for freezing any rise in fees, the universities' arguments for raising them; and will explore possible alternative funding mechanisms.

Ordering your arguments

Your aim here should be an effortless flow in the sequence of your evidence. The reader should feel that there is an intelligent mind at work here, sifting methodically through facts and figures to arrive at a sensible, logical conclusion. If you are planning an essay which will come down on one side of an argument, a practical template might be as follows:

An introduction in which both viewpoints are set out.
A first paragraph which develops ideas **contrary** to your viewpoint.
Subsequent paragraphs developing ideas **contrary** to your viewpoint.
A paragraph which develops ideas **coinciding** with your viewpoint.
Subsequent paragraphs with ideas which **coincide** with your viewpoint.
A conclusion summing up the competing evidence and making your stance clear.

Why this sequence? Your supportive conclusion follows on naturally from the case you have just been making in the final paragraphs. The contrary arguments have been distanced into earlier paragraphs and your own arguments are what the reader is left contemplating at the essay's close. And research shows that readers tend to remember the last evidence they have been given.

If you're planning to remain neutral, make sure your reasons for standing back bear scrutiny and don't just show you to be a ditherer. Is there insufficient evidence for a clear-cut conclusion? Is the situation too fluid for a current stance? Is the topic too subjective for an objective view of any kind?

Structuring a conclusion

- Your conclusion should briefly re-visit the main points/arguments. If you are supporting one side, it would be sensible to restate the reasons why your choice has been made. Vary your vocabulary this time round, employing well-chosen synonyms to give a freshness to your comments rather than simply redeployinng phrases from your introduction.

- Re-emphasise the importance of this topic to society today and tomorrow. What bearing does it have on our humanity or our society?

- Do NOT introduce new material at this late stage. It will only blur the focus of your carefully constructed arguments.

- If you can manage to refer back to a comment you made earlier on in the essay – or answer a question you raised – that would lend a certain stylistic elegance to your writing, suggesting a satisfyingly cyclical form to the text.

- As in your dissertation, you need to offer a bibliography of your sources.

 **DON'T FORGET**

Quality newspapers are a rich source of current hot topics suitable for argumentative essays. Their quoted experts or cited surveys could be googled to explore the relevant information in much greater depth.

 THINGS TO DO AND THINK ABOUT

If you're still casting around for a suitable topic, check out the 'debatabase' link on the Digital Zone. Read a few of the debates on culture, economy, education, environment, etc. Examine the points for and against a topic which interests you. This will give you leads to arguments but you will still have to conduct your own research from these leads if your essay is to offer convincing depth.

TEXTUAL ANALYSIS

WHAT ARE YOU BEING ASKED TO DO?

The quick answer? Nothing you haven't been doing for the past six years. In your English classes, you have been reading poems, novels, articles and plays ever since S1. You've been faced with all these genres in class tests and public exams. And you've coped well with answering questions on them, otherwise you wouldn't be a candidate for Advanced Higher English.

WHAT'S NEW?

Now, for the first time, you're being asked – under exam conditions – to give a detailed critical response to a text **you have never seen before**. Before panic sets in, remember that you can select a piece for comment from the genre in which you feel most at home: poetry, fiction, non-fiction or drama.

WHAT FORM WILL THE QUESTIONS TAKE?

Questions will vary according to the genre you have selected. For example, in poetry you may simply be asked to give a detailed critical response to a poem. In prose fiction, non-fiction and drama, you may be asked to comment on how an author achieves a specific effect through selected techniques or structuring. And, of course, you have been doing just that in your study of Scottish texts and other literature for Higher English.

WHAT FORM SHOULD YOUR CRITICAL ANALYSIS TAKE?

The good news is you're not obliged to write in critical essay form if you don't want to. You can choose to answer in linked paragraphs or extended bullet points. What's important is that whatever form your response takes, it should be appropriately structured to meet the full demands of your selected question. And, at this level, your response must demonstrate real depth of personal response as well as thorough technical knowledge. In other words, demonstrating **understanding**, **analysis** and **evaluation**.

HOW CAN YOU PREPARE FOR THE *TEXTUAL ANALYSIS* PAPER?

In the months leading up to the exam, you need to get in as much practice as possible in commenting on unseen texts in all four genres. This might take the form of written responses, discussions with a partner, or a class activity. Not only will this broaden your critical skills, but it will ensure that you'll have a decent choice of question in the exam. Remember, although poetry – for example – may be your genre of choice, the set poem on the day may not suit you as well as you had hoped, so it's always wise to ensure that you're capable of answering on an alternative genre.

HOW ADEQUATE IS YOUR CRITICAL VOCABULARY?

Poetry, fiction, non-fiction and drama, while sharing certain elements of critical vocabulary, have terms specific to each genre. You will need to be familiar with these if you're to discuss fluently your response to your chosen text.

contd

Textual Analysis: What are you being asked to do?

At Advanced Higher, you are now well beyond offering up intelligent generalities. Here, you must demonstrate a certain sophistication of critical language when discussing the complex texts with which you will be faced. Over the following pages, we'll be helping you to develop accuracy in employing critical terms.

WHAT EXACTLY IS A CRITICAL RESPONSE?

After reading your selected text and its accompanying question, you'll need to ask yourself what the author appears to be attempting to convey, how effectively (in your opinion) they convey it, and what means they use. Make sure your response to the incident/experience (and the wording of the question) is amply supported by detailed analysis. In other words, you'll need to pinpoint what seems to you to be the text's main ideas (and the question's focus) and then respond with your own reaction, backing all of this up with plenty of relevant textual evidence. But be careful, glibness with technical terms will not conceal a lack of personal response.

DON'T FORGET

Textual analysis is as much about you as it is about the text in front of you.

ONLINE

For more on 'writing the critical response', head to www.brightredbooks.net Here, you'll find a link with advice for a full-scale critical response essay, but what this piece has to say about 'analysing (interpretation and evaluation)' is particularly useful for writing extended bullet points.

THINGS TO DO AND THINK ABOUT

Success in the *Textual Analysis* paper draws on the reading skills you've been developing throughout your school career. The major difference now is that the text you'll be faced with is one which you have not seen before.

To get used to this idea, take a short poem you have never read (from a standard school anthology) and ask yourself the following:

- What is the poem about?
- How does it make you feel?
- How do the poet's techniques help you to reach these feelings?

Work with a partner; take notes; and compare them. Did you both comment on the same or different features? What is your partner's assessment of the poem? Does it differ from yours? If so, how does it differ?

One of Shakespeare's sonnets would be a good place to start.

TIP: Check out what's going on in each stanza and how these stanzas relate to the final two lines. And don't panic! We'll work on one together shortly. But it'll be good to see how you get on at your first attempt.

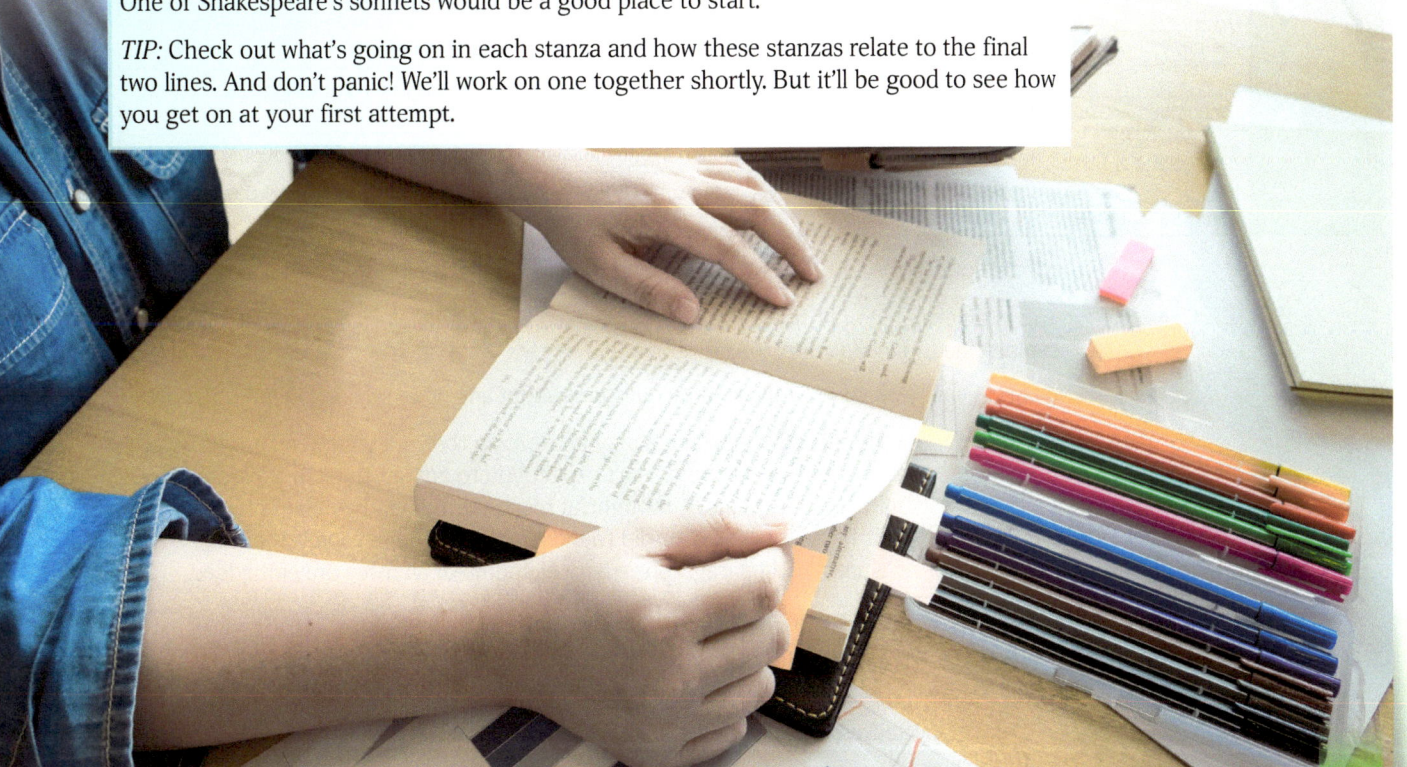

59

TEXTUAL ANALYSIS

COMMENTING ON POETRY

DON'T FORGET

For exam success, these terms need to be firmly in your head as well as your file. But, remember, you won't be expected to touch on every one of these terms in every single answer. Choose only the most appropriate for the set task.

HOW WELL DO YOU KNOW THE TERMS?

A mark-winning critical appreciation of a poem must offer not only an engaged personal response but an appropriate use of technical language. Let's see how familiar you are with some of the more common terms you'll need.

ACTIVITY

Here are some definitions of common terms used when discussing poems. These offer a useful basis for your critical response. Match the definition on the right with the correct term on the left.

1. voice/persona	a) A poem has a _____ _____ when a recurring pattern of lines and stanzas is immediately apparent. Some of the most common _____ _____ are sonnets and ballads. Some fine effects can be created when the poet interrupts the _____ _____.
2. imagery	b) _____ _____ is poetry liberated from the constraints of regular form and fixed metre. Although avoiding repeating patterns of lines and stanzas, the poet may sometimes still use rhyme and rhythm to achieve specific effects.
3. rhythm	c) A _____ is a group of lines within a poem. There is no set length to a _____ nor do they have to be the same length. A _____ of two lines is called a couplet; one of three lines a tercet; one of four lines a quatrain.
4. sound devices	d) _____ or _____ is the character adopted by the speaker in a poem. Detecting clues to the attitude or point of view of the _____ or _____ speaking will enrich your response greatly.
5. mood	e) _____ _____ refers to the writer's selection of vocabulary. Often this is based not simply on denotational values but, more tellingly, on connotative associations.
6. word choice	f) _____ is the name given to pictures in words triggered by the senses of sight, touch, hearing, taste and smell. It covers various devices such as metaphors, similes, personification, onomatopoeia, etc. (See *BrightRED CfE Higher English Study Guide* p. 14 for definitions of these terms.)
7. tone	g) _____ is the repetition of the end-sounds of words.
8. free verse	h) _____ is the regular pattern of sound (or beat), most audible when a poem's read aloud. Some of the common patterns are iambic, trochaic, anapaestic and dactylic. Poets may break any of these patterns to create a specific effect.
9. rhyme	i) _____ is the emphasis that falls on some syllables and not others. How this _____ is arranged within the poem is the basis of poetic rhythm. Poets may sometimes break the stress pattern to create particular effects.
10. stress	j) _____ _____ are what poets use to convey and reinforce the meaning or experience when denotation and connotation are not quite enough. Popular forms are alliteration, onomatopoeia, assonance, etc.
11. stanza	k) _____ is the creation of certain feelings in readers through the manipulation of words or devices for emotional effect.
12. regular form(s)	l) _____ is the unspoken attitude of a writer towards the subject. It's generally made clear through word choice, rhythm and imagery. (See *Bright Red CfE Higher English Study Guide* pp. 22–23.)

MAKING THE TERMS WORK FOR YOU

Ask yourself these three questions about any poem which you may encounter:

- What is the poem about?
- By what means has the poet shaped my response?
- What is my response to the poem?

Although these questions may be running through your head as you read, your critical response doesn't expect you to answer them in separate, water-tight compartments. A thoughtful response may find you demonstrating your familiarity with our old friends – understanding, analysis and evaluation – in paragraphs where elements of all three are embedded.

A poem in regular form

Using the poetic literary terms we've examined here, let's use the three questions to help us explore and comment on interesting features of Shakespeare's 'Sonnet No. 12'.

contd

Textual Analysis: Commenting on poetry

1. **What is this poem about?** (show your **understanding**)
The theme appears to be about the passing of time and its harmful ageing process. The speaker observes how the passing of time corrupts the beauties of nature before turning his attention to the beauty of the person being addressed, suggesting that the only way to preserve his beauty is to have children to perpetuate his present attractiveness.

2. **By what means has the poet shaped my response** (showing your **analysis**)

Voice: There is an 'I' present in the first three quatrains who, in the third, turns his attention to 'thy beauty' and 'thee' in the couplet, suggesting the speaker and addressee are on friendly, familiar terms.

Structure: The poet chooses to employ three quatrains and a final couplet to shape his ideas into three distinct phases. These phases are shaped by the opening word in each quatrain: 'When ...', 'When ...', 'Then ...'

> SONNET No. 12
> When I do count the clock that tells the time,
> And see the brave day sunk in hideous night;
> When I behold the violet past prime,
> And sable curls all silver'd oe'r with white;
>
> When lofty trees I see barren of leaves
> Which erst from heat did canopy the herd,
> And summer's green all girded up in sheaves
> Borne on the bier with white and bristly beard,
>
> Then of thy beauty do I question make,
> That thou amongst the wastes of time must go,
> Since sweets and beauties do themselves forsake
> And die as fast as they see others grow;
>
> And nothing 'gainst Time's scythe can make defence
> Save breed, to brave him when he takes thee hence.

The first quatrain lists the depressing effect of the passing of time on day (which turns into 'hideous night'); on beautiful flowers like violets, which wither; and on 'sable' black hair which turns silvery white. In other words, the degrading effect of time over days, weeks and years. The second quatrain opens out the inspection of decay on nature in general: trees become 'barren of leaves' and green crops eventually turn white to be cut down and carried away, 'borne on the bier' like a human corpse. This latter image hints at a link between the life of nature and man himself. When confronted with this brutally uncomfortable reminder of human mortality, the speaker then turns to his addressee and his beauty in the third quatrain: 'Then of thy beauty do I question make' before turning in the concluding couplet to the only solution he envisages for perpetuating his addressee's beauty: to have children.

Imagery: The overarching image is one of the corrupting power of time over the life of humans and nature, summed up by 'the wastes of time' and 'Time's scythe'. Human life is envisaged, like the cornfield, as subject to ripening and then cutting down before being finally 'borne on the bier'.

Word Choice: Words and phrases such as 'hideous night' (darkness), 'barren of leaves' (nakedness), 'borne on the bier' (death) and 'wastes of time' (emptiness) reinforce with their connotations of sterility and death the frighteningly destructive power of passing time.

Rhythm: In the first line, the stress falls on words like 'I', 'count', 'clock', 'tells', and 'time', which suggests the relentless tick-tock of a clock measuring out our life implacably. The continuation of this stress pattern (weak/strong or iambic pentameter, to use the more technical term) throughout the sonnet underlines the dominant theme of time's relentless and destructive march.

3. **What is my response to the poem?** (showing your **evaluation** and **appreciation**)
The use of three quatrains and a couplet to shape the stages of his thought sees Shakespeare creating for us a perfect marriage between structure and meaning. The 'When's followed by the 'Then' guide us carefully to the poet's only solution to the challenge of time. By paralleling the life of nature and man in highly visual and seasonal terms, the passing of time is brought home to readers with great graphic force. Adding to this is the relentless stress pattern of the lines (weak/strong) which evokes the sound of a clock ticking off the hours of human life. Imagery, rhythm and structure work together to offer readers not just a satisfying unity of ideas but a novel way, perhaps, to fend off the ravages of time.

 **DON'T FORGET**

In a work of art where form and meaning are so inextricably interwoven, it's almost inevitable that the line between analysis and evaluation/appreciate will become blurred. Your examiners are aware of this, too!

 ONLINE

For a fuller description of analysis points, head to www.brightredbooks.net

 THINGS TO DO AND THINK ABOUT

Choose another poem with formalised rhythm and rhyme. Working with a partner, explore how structure and meaning are employed to create a satisfying unity. How has the material been divided up? How is this structure guiding the reader through the poet's experience? Which technical terms would be appropriate for comment in your bullet points? Remember, comments need to reveal understanding, analysis and evaluation.

TEXTUAL ANALYSIS

FORMAL STRUCTURES AND THEIR USEFULNESS

Why, over the centuries, have so many poets chosen to write in formal, readily recognisable structures? What advantages do set formats in stanza patterns and rhyme schemes offer authors and readers?

THE BENEFITS OF FORM

A recognised poetic form, with a pre-determined shape and regular rhyme scheme, creates a tight framework both for the poet's ideas and the reader's expectations.

Fulfilling expectations

Often, the verses or stanzas within the framework will each deal with a specific aspect of the topic. Formality of this kind gives a reassuring sense of organisation. We saw how Shakespeare in Sonnet 12 used two quatrains to deal with the ravages of passing time in general before turning, in the third quatrain, to the personal consequences of this process on his friend. Finally, in the couplet, he offers a solution to the problem. Readers here are aware of a structuring hand at work, which helps guide them through the sequence of the poet's thoughts. The patterning gives a comforting sense of direction for the journey on which they're being taken.

But it's not only ideas that a set stanza pattern can help organise. Narrated events can also be made to be more readily followed when a recurring pattern of lines and rhymes is employed. A common format of ballads – four lines following an *a/b/c/b* rhyme scheme – allows a ballad narrative to unfold clearly, while at the same time fulfilling the reader's rhythmic expectations. We see this at work in the opening of 'The Ballad of Sir Patrick Spens':

> *The king sits in Dunfermline town,*
> *Drinkin the blude-reid wine*
> *'O whaur will A get a skeely skipper,*
> *Tae sail this new ship o mine?'*
>
> *O up and spak an eldern knight,*
> *Sat at the king's richt knee:*
> *'Sir Patrick Spens is the best sailor*
> *That ever sailt the sea.'*

The pleasing predictability of structure and rhyme drives on the narrative flow to the benefit of poet and reader alike.

Confounding expectations

Sometimes, poets deliberately break the patterns they have set up to draw attention to a change of mood or atmosphere. The first two verses of Thomas Hardy's 'The Man He Killed' tell how a soldier in the First World War follows orders and fires at the enemy. They initially follow a regular stress pattern:

> *'Had he and I but met*
>   *By some old ancient inn,*
> *We should have sat us down to wet*
>   *Right many a nipperkin!*
>
> *'But ranged as infantry,*
>   *And staring face to face,*
> *I shot at him as he at me,*
>   *And killed him in his place.*

contd

Textual Analysis: Formal structures and their usefulness

However, the next verse has a broken, halting stress pattern, emphasised by punctuation quite different from that in the earlier two stanzas. It suggests the soldier's growing unease about his orders. Note, too, how 'although' is stressed to rhyme with 'foe', as if there is now increasing doubt about his opponent's status as an enemy:

> 'I shot him dead because –
>   Because he was my foe,
> Just so: my foe, of course he was;
>   That's clear enough; although

When giving a response to a poem, any break from predictable patterning, whether in line structure or stress, may help you to detect a change of direction in the poet or speaker's thoughts. As such, it is well worth examining fully and commenting on.

 **DON'T FORGET**

A personal response may see you reacting to your text in several ways – amused, moved, surprised, or perhaps provoked into thinking about something familiar in a new way. Whatever your response, ensure there is always a personal dimension present in your answer ... and support it with compelling evidence.

THE IMPORTANCE OF STRESS

When we talk about rhythm in discussing poetry, we are noting that certain syllables are stressed while others are not. Any analysis of a poem would do well to consider the pattern of stressed and unstressed syllables, for this is the basis of rhythm. And the rhythm selected by the poet is a key element in determining mood, atmosphere and attitude. Just as the 'beat' is important in determining the mood in a piece of music, so, too, is the stress pattern in a line of poetry.

Stressed or unstressed?

If we look again at Shakespeare's Sonnet No. 12, we see the following pattern of stressed and unstressed syllables at work ('⌣' is unstressed; '–' is stressed):

> ⌣ – | ⌣ – | ⌣ – | ⌣ – | ⌣ –
> When I do count the clock that tells the time,

This 'da-dum' (weak–strong) pattern is popular in poetry. Note that there are five of these 'da-dums' in each line of the sonnet. Each 'da-dum' is called a foot or, more precisely, a metrical foot. (Musicians among you know that music is divided up into bars; poetry is divided up into metrical feet.) Each foot of a line tends to follow a certain stress pattern. The proper name for the 'da-dum' foot is an **iamb**. Since there are five of these iambs in the sonnet line, we call this pattern an **iambic pentameter**.

THINGS TO DO AND THINK ABOUT

Re-read Shakespeare's Sonnet No. 12. Look in particular at the stress patterns in the couplet. How do the stresses here focus our attention on Shakespeare's advice to his friend? Are there other places in the sonnet where the stresses seem to be particularly interesting?

ONLINE

Find more on the importance of rhythm and rhyme in poetry at www.brightredbooks.net

TEXTUAL ANALYSIS

FORMAL STRUCTURES: RHYTHM AND RHYME

RHYTHM

We've discovered that Shakespeare's sonnet was structured around the iamb to give each line an iambic pentameter format. The iamb is one of the more common rhythmic patterns. In discussing poetry, you will encounter several others. Let's look in a little more detail at some you may find useful.

An **iamb** is formed from a 'weak–strong' beat ('⌣' '—') or 'da-dum'. Its adjective is 'iambic'.	A **trochee** is the very reverse of an iamb, offering a 'strong–weak' beat ('—' '⌣') or 'dum-da'. Its adjective is 'trochaic'.
An **anapaest** (or anapest) is formed by two 'weaks' followed by a 'strong' ('⌣⌣' '—') or 'da-da-dum'. Its adjective is 'anapaestic' or 'anapestic'.	A **dactyl** is the reverse of an anapaest, following a 'strong–weak–weak' pattern ('—' '⌣⌣') or 'dum-da-da'. Its adjective is 'dactylic'.

There are other rhythmic patterns in metrical feet which you may encounter. Have a look at www.thepoetryarchive.com for more details.

Remember, however, it's not the naming of these metrical patterns which will gain the praise of your examiners; you must pinpoint the effect that the rhythm contributes to the reading experience. Never lose sight of that.

Counting feet

We saw that five iambs in a line gave us what we call an iambic pentameter ('penta' being Greek for five). Here are some of the more common terms to account for the number of metrical feet in a line.

A line with 3 metrical feet is called a **trimeter**.	A line with 4 metrical feet is called a **tetrameter**.
A line with 5 metrical feet is called a **pentameter**.	A line with 6 metrical feet is called a **hexameter**.

Lines with more than six are pretty rare. From time to time, you may encounter dimeters (two feet).

Allow for flexibility

Poetry, like music, is an art form. While music's 'beat' and poetry's metrical feet create an underlying rhythmic pattern to the content, an art form is never robotic. Ruthless following of a set rhythmic pattern leads to monotony.

You'll find that, just as music speeds up or slows down, so do lines of poetry. While poets may favour, say, an underlying iambic line, you could find the odd anapaest sneaking in (or vice versa). You may also find a variation in the number of metrical feet to a line. This is perfectly normal and could be there to help emphasise a particular word or idea on which the poet wants us to focus.

Working with rhythm

Look at these four examples. Identify the underlying rhythmic pattern at work. (Remember about flexibility.) Say, too, how the rhythmic pattern affects the reading experience. What does this rhythm make you feel? (This is the most important part of the exercise!) If you're feeling ambitious, try to determine the underlying number of feet – pentameter, tetrameter, etc.

> He it was who sent the wood-birds,
> Sent the Shawshaw, sent the swallow,
> Sent the wild-goose, Wawa, northward,
> Sent the melons and tobacco,
> And the grapes in purple clusters.

Longfellow, H. W. 'Song of Hiawatha'

> The Assyrian came down like a wolf on the fold,
> And his cohorts were gleaming in purple and gold;
> And the sheen of their spears was like stars on the sea,
> When the blue wave rolls nightly on deep Galilee.

Byron, G. G. 'The Destruction of Sennacherib'

> Half a league, half a league,
> Half a league onward,
> All in the valley of Death
> Rode the six hundred.
> 'Forward the Light Brigade!
> Charge for the guns!' he said
> Into the valley of Death
> Rode the six hundred.

Tennyson, A. L. 'The Charge of the Light Brigade'

> I wandered, lonely as a cloud
> That floats on high o'er dales and hills
> When, all at once, I saw a crowd,
> A host of golden daffodils
> Beside the lake, beneath the trees,
> Fluttering and dancing in the breeze.

Wordsworth, W. 'I Wandered Lonely as a Cloud'

Textual Analysis: Formal structures: rhythm and rhyme

RHYME

Rhyme is when a poet deliberately repeats the end-sound of certain lines to match the sound of other lines in a verse. We usually call this pattern a rhyme scheme. We identify it by giving similar sounding end-words the same letter:

Is my team ploughing,	a
That I was used to drive	b
And hear the harness jingle	c
When I was man alive?	b
Ay, the horses trample,	d
The harness jingles now;	e
No change though you lie under	f
The land you used to plough.	e

Housman, A. E. 'Is My Team Ploughing'

How it supports rhythm

One critic, Kayla Giesbrecht, has suggested that 'Rhythm is the pulse of poetry, and rhyme is its echo'. Once you have detected the mood of the rhythm, you may find that the sound of the rhyme intensifies that mood. As such, rhyme supports rhythm to make a poem a musical, as well as an emotional, experience.

Quite often, the **sense** of the words that perform the rhyme add much to the atmosphere of the verse. For example:

> I leant upon a coppice gate
>   When Frost was spectre grey,
> And Winter's dregs made desolate
>   The weakening eye of day.

Hardy, T. 'The Darkling Thrush'

'Grey' rhymes with 'day'; 'and gate' with 'desolate', emphasising a grim bleakness of mood and landscape. In other words, rhyme can intensify the focus on a particular point to great effect. We notice this in Hardy's 'The Man He Killed':

> 'I shot him dead because–
>   Because he was my foe,
> Just so: my foe, of course he was;
>   That's clear enough, although

Hardy, T. 'The Man He Killed'

The rhyme falling on both 'foe' and 'although' hints at the speaker's increasing doubt that his opponent is a true enemy.

Half-rhyme

Sometimes, poets like the framework of a rhyme scheme but don't want the rhymes to dominate too much. They 'tone down' the rhyme by using half-rhyme at line ends to make them less noticeable. A half-rhyme is a rhyme in which the rhyming words are close but not identical to each other. For example:

> When have I last looked **on**
> The round green eyes and the long wavering **bodies**
> Of the dark leopards of the **moon?**
> All the wild witches, those most noble **ladies** ...

Yeats, W. B. 'Lines Written in Dejection'

At times, poets exploit enjambment to add a conversational tone to lines not 'end-stopped' by full rhyme. For example:

> That is no country for old men. The **young**
> In one another's arms, birds in the trees
> – Those dying generations – at their **song,**

Yeats, W. B. 'Sailing to Byzantium'

THINGS TO DO AND THINK ABOUT

To explore the technical aspects of formal poetry in more detail, read 'The Close Reading of Poetry' on the Digital Zone. This informative account will give you confidence when discussing poetry. But remember, citing technical features is something you do to support your personal response. It's not a substitute for one.

DON'T FORGET

If in doubt about the stress patterns in a poem, say it aloud. This is the best way to hear which syllables are stressed or unstressed.

ONLINE

Find more about rhythm patterns at www.brightredbooks.net

TEXTUAL ANALYSIS

FREE VERSE AND COHESION

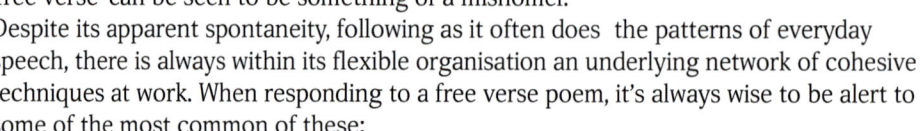

If poems were to be unshackled from the constraints of recurring rhyme schemes and regular rhythmic patterns, what, then, would poets put in their place to create a unified work of art?

Around the end of the nineteenth and the beginning of the twentieth century, this question saw a number of answers from key figures such as Walt Whitman, T. S. Eliot and Ezra Pound. However, examined closely, 'free verse' can be seen to be something of a misnomer. Despite its apparent spontaneity, following as it often does the patterns of everyday speech, there is always within its flexible organisation an underlying network of cohesive techniques at work. When responding to a free verse poem, it's always wise to be alert to some of the most common of these:

- internal rhyme
- unifying imagery
- caesura
- symbolism
- alliteration
- personification
- word associations
- assonance
- enjambment
- contrast

FREE VERSE UNPICKED

One early poet working in free verse, who influenced the rather better-known T. S. Eliot, is T. E. Hulme. An early exponent of this form, Hulme realised a number, but not all, of the key features mentioned above in this poem about a homeless person.

The Embankment

(The fantasia of a fallen gentleman on a cold, bitter night)
Once, in finesse of fiddles found I ecstasy,
In a flash of gold heels on the hard pavement.
Now see I
That warmth's the very stuff of poesy.
Oh, God, make small
The old star-eaten blanket of the sky,
That I may fold it round me and in comfort lie.

Hulme, T. E. 'The Embankment', https://www.poetryfoundation.org/poems/44432/the-embankment

A casual reading might overlook the craftsmanship which conceals itself well beneath a seemingly spontaneous outpouring of feeling. But, when we analyse the poem a little further, we can see that this very short lyric employs a number of features to create a satisfying unity. Let's look at some of these:

TECHNIQUE	EFFECT
Internal rhyme – 'cold', 'gold', 'old' and 'fold'	From the subtitle onwards, there's a chain of internal rhymes which encapsulate much of the speaker's experience – both in the past and present. A sequence of events in the homeless man's life is hinted at in **assonance**. This chain also helps shape the poem itself.
Alliteration – 'fantasia of a fallen gentleman', 'in finesse of fiddles found I '	The alliteration on 'f' binds together both the speaker's present situation and his past life, helping us feel for ourselves his contrasting experiences.
Contrast – 'Once' and 'Now'	The 'Once' and the 'Now' shape the poem into a 'then' and 'now' format, underlining the speaker's vastly altered values – and status.

contd

Textual Analysis: Free verse and cohesion

Imagery – 'the finesse of fiddles', 'flash of gold heels', 'star-eaten blanket'	The first two emphasise most economically the flashy lifestyle once enjoyed by the speaker: dances/concerts and smartly dressed women – the world of society.
	The 'star-eaten blanket' is what he would be happy to settle for in his now solitary life. Sound and sight are suddenly less important than the comforting, warming touch of the blanket. Notice, too, how one set of images ('fiddles' and 'heels') takes everyday items and sets them in contrast to the infinite 'star-eaten' blanket of the heavens.
Word associations – 'star-eaten', 'stuff of poesy'	'Moth-eaten' is perhaps the word we would be quickest to associate with blankets. Hulme has taken this common expression and turned it into a vivid image with the blanket now being eaten into by stars rather than by moths.
	He also exploits the associations we make with 'stuff': yes, subject matter of poetry, but it also has fabric associations for the man seeking comfort from his 'star-eaten' blanket.
Enjambment	The conversational tone of the poem benefits from enjambment at several points, giving the impression simply of a man mulling over his past and present state.

DON'T FORGET

Note that poets writing in free verse don't necessarily forsake rhythm and rhyme entirely. (Hulme chooses to round off 'The Embankment' with a final rhyming couplet.) In free verse, rhyme and rhythm are no longer the organising instruments of a poem's structure, rather just two of many literary techniques and devices which poets may, or may not, use to bring unity to their work.

THINGS TO DO AND THINK ABOUT

Here, the poet writes of 'the blues' he suffers from by being separated from the woman he loves. At first sight, it may appear like a spontaneous outpouring of his emotion. On closer inspection, however, we see that the poet has carefully constructed a framework of ideas and images to give external form to his inner feelings.

The Blues
The lights are on all over Hamilton.
The sky is dark, blue
as a stained-glass window in an unfrequented church
say, by Chagall, with grand and glorious chinks
of pinks and purples,
glittering jewels on those glass-fronted buildings
where lifts are all descending
and the doors are being closed.
    You're out there somewhere,
going to a concert in wide company or maybe
sitting somewhere weaving a carpet
like a giant tapestry, coloured grey,
pale brown, weaving the wool
back in at the edges of the frame, your
fingers deft as they turn the wool in tight and
gentle curves.
    Or somewhere else.
    What do I do
    except imagine you?
    The river I keep crossing
    keeps going north. The trains
    in the night cross it too.
    Their silver carriages are blue.

Riach, A. (1991) 'The Blues', *This Folding Map*, Auckland, Auckland University Press

Working with a partner, take notes on the above poem with a view to writing a detailed critical response. Remember to cover **understanding, analysis and evaluation** in your comments. You will have many thoughts of your own here, but if you're having difficulty getting started, consider these few features and what they bring to the reading experience:

- The network of colour references
- Imagery/extended simile
- Contrast of language
- Enjambment
- Alliteration
- Change of pace

ONLINE

Find notes to accompany this task for teaching or self-marking at www.brightredbooks.net

TEXTUAL ANALYSIS
COMMENTING ON PROSE FICTION

Here, as in poetry, you must offer an engaged personal response as well as demonstrating appropriate use of technical language. You'll usually be invited to discuss the effectiveness of the writer's presentation of some feature of the text. In doing so, you need to show understanding, analysis and evaluation.

The good news is, much of the work you have put into studying and responding to poetry and RUAE will pay dividends when discussing prose fiction. Rhythm and rhyme will be taking a back seat for now, but the list of technical terms with which you need to be conversant is beginning to look rather familiar.

USEFUL TECHNICAL TERMS

narrative voice	characterisation
mood	tone
evocation of setting	word choice
imagery	sentence structure
theme	contrast
symbolism	structure

FIRST PERSON		THIRD PERSON*	
Advantages – We are allowed into the narrator's innermost thoughts and feelings. We come close to them by seeing the world through their eyes. 'I', 'my' 'we', and 'our' are obviously the favoured pronouns.	**Limitations** – We cannot know what others in the text may be thinking.	**Advantages** – Narrative unfolds as seen through the eyes and comments of a certain character in the story. Readers are often expected to sympathise with this character's viewpoint.	**Limitations** – Readers are not always aware of what other characters may be thinking or feeling.

* Sometimes, a third-person narrator is not an individual character in the text but an all-knowing, 'authorial' voice which focuses on the lives of all the characters, but merely as an onlooker. Sometimes this is referred to as the 'I-am-a-camera' technique.

In writing novels or short stories, writers all share one major aim: to create an experience for readers which mirrors exactly what the writer felt as they imagined the story. Their aim is the creation of a wholly convincing world in which readers lose themselves entirely until the very last line. Characterisation, setting, language, plotting and thematic development are central to this creation. As magical as their world may be, its successful creation is rooted in skilful deployment of many of the terms in the above grid. That's why your personal response to the text and question must be alert to how these terms contribute to the text's realisation.

Let's discuss these technical terms and explore their contribution.

Narrative voice

In prose fiction, narrative voice is usually either in the first or third person. (Second-person narrative does exist but it's relatively rare – for an example see parts of Iain Banks' *Complicity*.) How does each voice affect the narrative?

Characterisation

Here's a brief checklist of points to look out for in the presentation of characters in prose fiction.

Role	Are they the narrator?
	Are they the hero/heroine?
	Are they the villain?
	If neither narrator/hero/villain, why present in story?
	What is their initial impact on the reader?
	What creates this impact? Behaviour to others/ treatment by others/author's description/ dialogue?
	Does our view of them change?
Personality	Age? Appearance? Behavioural traits/quirks?
	What are their strengths?
	What are their weaknesses?
	What impact does this personality have on the reader? What creates this reaction in the reader?
	Do they change throughout the action?

ONLINE

For interesting comments on narrative voice, see the link on the Digital Zone. This is also useful for your own creative writing.

contd

Textual Analysis: Commenting on prose fiction

Relationships	Who are their friends?
	Do they *have* friends?
	Are they contrasted with anyone else?
	What contrasts do you observe?
	Are they in conflict with anyone? If so, who and why?
Behaviour in key incidents	How do their actions here reveal their character?
	What are their private thoughts here?
	How do their actions affect others?
	Are we told anecdotes about past behaviour?

Setting

Setting contributes greatly to the tone that the writer is attempting to establish. It also impacts on the mood evoked in the reader.

Physical	When do the events happen?
	Over what time scale?
	Is landscape/townscape/homescape important to the narrative?
	How do word choice, imagery and sentence structure contribute to the setting's description?
	What changes of scene are there?
	Are weather conditions important?
	Does changing weather affect the morale of character?
	Are there recurring references, for example, to heat, cold, water, colour, etc.?
	Why might the writer have used these?
Society	What level of society does the character find themselves in? Rich? Poor? Does this change?
	What kind of society surrounds the character? Settled? Conflicted?
	Do they fit in?
	Do they encounter other types of society?
	How do they react to them?

Language

While clues to tone and mood may be evoked in setting, tone and mood are more directly addressed in the language of the narrative.

Word choice	Is the author content to employ words for their purely denotative meaning?
	Or are they exploiting their underlying connotations?
	Is the word choice encountered in everyday life? Or is it more poetic/academic?
	What impact does this word choice have on the reader?

Imagery	Do metaphors, similes, personification and devices such as alliteration and onomatopoeia play a part in the language of the text? If so, to what effect? How might a reader react?
Symbolism	Are there items which seem to have a greater significance than their surface appearance? For example, a withered rose, a broken glass, a white dove, etc.? How might these affect readers?
Sentence structure	Is the writer employing a conversational approach to sentence structure, with short or incomplete statements? Or, is the sentence structure suggesting a more formal/detached tone? How might the writer's adopted approach affect the reader's response? To what extent does it invite reader engagement?

Plotting/narrative structure

Plot is perhaps a term best reserved for novels, but short stories require a framing narrative structure. Commenting on this is a key feature of any exploration of a short story.

Organisation	Does the narrative unfold chronologically?
	Does the narrative employ flashbacks?
	Is there a cyclical movement? That is, does the narrative end where it started?
	Are all loose ends tied up?
Narrative style	From whose viewpoint is the story told?
	Is there more than one narrator?
	Are there important action-provoking key scenes?
	Why are they important? What do we learn from them? What are the consequences for the characters – and the plot?

Theme(s)

In even the briefest short story, a writer will hint at an underlying idea or theme. It's often this which will have triggered it being written in the first place. Remember, plot is what happens in the story; theme is what the story is **about**.

Social/ historical	What is being suggested about the society (or societies) described? Greedy, narrow-minded, prejudiced, unfeeling, etc.?
	What evidence have you for saying this?
	How does this evidence emerge? Key incidents/events? Conversations? Conflicts?
Personal/ moral	Are there personality characteristics that people may share in their dealings with others? Are they generous, tolerant, repressed, etc.?
	What evidence have you for saying this?
	How does this evidence emerge? Key incidents/events? Conversations? Conflicts?

THINGS TO DO AND THINK ABOUT

Working with a partner, select a short story you haven't already read in class. Make notes as you read. Then split the topics in the above grids between you. (Narrative voice, characterisation, etc.) Try to answer those questions appropriate to your selected story. Point to specific incidents/conversations/descriptions to support your bullet points. Are there other points, not covered in the grid, that you noticed?

TEXTUAL ANALYSIS
NON-FICTION PROSE

As in prose fiction, you will usually be invited to discuss the effectiveness of the writer's presentation of some feature of the text. In doing so, you will remember, of course, to show **understanding**, **analysis** and **evaluation**.

Writers in this genre share the same desire as fiction writers – the creation of a rich reading experience. Although using many of the same techniques as prose fiction, they take their material from life experience and real-world events, rather than purely from their imagination.

While entertaining, they also describe and inform. The genre encompasses many text-types, including:

- travel writing
- biographies/autobiographies
- political sketches
- literary essays
- feature articles.

CHARACTERISTICS

Candidates who are familiar with the techniques described in the prose fiction section of this guide will already be well equipped to discuss prose non-fiction. However, to intensify the effectiveness of their descriptions and views, they might usefully spend time considering some of the more popular linguistic techniques favoured by writers in this genre.

Sensory detail – vital where vividness of description is sought.	**Imagery/figurative language** – key when graphic detail is targeted.	**Contrast** – useful for highlighting changed situations/fortunes.
Varied sentence structure – keeps narrative moving forward and reader interest alive.	**Common features in non-fiction prose**	**Tone** – whether humorous or serious, the writer's 'persona' is usually prominent.
Structure – variable, dependent on topic; carefully sequenced for continuing reader engagement. Beginning and end often linked.	**Narrative voice** – first person narrative common, with writer's personality usually well to the fore.	**Word choice** – a reliable clue to writer's stance, for example, 'freedom fighter' or 'terrorist'.

DON'T FORGET

Check out the thrust of the question before you start reading the passage. This will help focus your underlining on only the most relevant items for comment. Too much underlining will be bewildering when you come to write up your response; too few will lead to a slender answer.

Textual Analysis: Non-fiction prose

 THINGS TO DO AND THINK ABOUT

Commenting on non-fiction prose

Here is a short extract from a book by a food writer. The question is of the kind you might well expect to meet in the exam room.

> *Discuss how effectively Sterling conveys to us the impact of this personal experience. You may wish to consider:*
>
> - *structure*
> - *contrast*
> - *his realisation of the 'sepulchral' nature of the dining room.*
>
> In the sepulchral dining room, I took a seat near the entry. As I waited in the thick, dim gloom, I wondered what ghosts might look like. I could almost hear the echoes of tinkling crystal, the clatter of china, the hum and buzz of conversation as deals were struck, information was exchanged and successes and failures recounted.
>
> I suddenly became aware of the old waiter standing beside me. The menu he brought me was English to the bone: meat, fish, boiled potatoes. At the waiter's suggestion I ordered steamed sole. As I waited to be served, I realised that there were others in the room. On the far side were an Indian man and a Chinese woman. I couldn't figure how they got there without my noticing. I had sat near the entry so I would be aware of anyone coming or going. They were sitting shoulder to shoulder and were in a whispered and animated, but deliberately subdued argument.
>
> When the sole arrived I found it bland, insipid, uninspired; fit food for ghosts. 'This is like eating death,' I thought. 'I need food for the living.' I caught the waiter's attention and the old bag of bones shuffled over my way. 'This is … very nice,' I said, referring to the meal. 'But isn't there anything on the menu with a little bit of … spice?'
>
> 'Pickled eggs, sir?' he suggested.
>
> 'I was thinking of something spicy hot.'
>
> He excused himself and disappeared into the kitchen. He soon returned to say, rather apologetically, that 'Cook is fixing himself and staff a bit of Malay curry if …'
>
> 'I'll take it!'
>
> He returned with a blue Chinese porcelain bowl filled with cubes of snowy white potato and toasty brown peanuts swimming in a thick, red-flecked yellow sauce. A sheen of red chilli-scented oil floated on top and a sprig of green cilantro graced it at the edge. He set it in front of me, ceremoniously turned the bowl 90 degrees, then shuffled quietly away.
>
> The vapours rose up and stung my nostrils. The smells of chilli, garlic and ginger were sharp and powerful. The buttery smell of peanut and the mellowness of turmeric combined with them as they formed an almost visible wreath around my head. I ignored the spoon and picked up the bowl with both hands. I sucked at the creamy sauce. Savoury spicefire rushed through my mouth, tiny beads of sweat popped from my brow, and my pallet sang: 'Alive!' I had sucked in a small piece of chilli so I bit into it and it burst into an explosion of flavourheat. I swallowed and the glow went down to my gut and it screamed: 'Alive. Alive. Alive!' I took up the spoon and scooped curry into my mouth and chewed. The capsicum struck my taste buds and they resonated like tiny tuning forks, each one a different tone, all together in harmony, a resounding air that kept the ghosts at bay.
>
> As I reached the bottom of the bowl I tipped it up and let the last tasty, searing bits slide into my mouth. Had the bowl been shallower I'd have licked it. The curry was so hot my mouth throbbed with a burning, life-affirming pleasure-pain. I felt like the only man of flesh in a cold charnel house.
>
> Sterling, R. (2001) 'The Fearless Diner' from *The Fire Never Dies*, Travelers' Tales

 DON'T FORGET

Ensure that the evidence you select to answer your exam question is wholly relevant. If the question focuses, say, on tension, only underline items which may support this. Tension could be realised under several grid headings. Keep a check-list of all of them in your head.

 ONLINE

Find notes to accompany this task for teaching or self-marking at www.brightredbooks.net

TEXTUAL ANALYSIS

COMMENTING ON DRAMA

Much of what has been said about the textual analysis of poetry, prose fiction and non-fiction can be applied to the exploration of drama: here, character, setting and plot require just as much examination and comment. But unlike these former genres, a play is much more than words on a page.

WHAT YOU NEED TO CONSIDER

DON'T FORGET

In the exam, you will be directed to commenting on some aspect of a scene. To save precious time, have a quick look at the question first. Then underline appropriately.

Your comments on drama need to take into consideration the demands of presenting a text in the context of a stage. Now, narrative is conveyed by more than words of dialogue. Successful play-presentation requires the full range of theatrical resources to be brought into play – to flesh out the text and project it three-dimensionally. Successful comment on a drama text requires candidates to be equally alert to the contributions made by resources such as:

- stage directions
- lighting
- props.
- costume
- music

What to look out for in character presentation

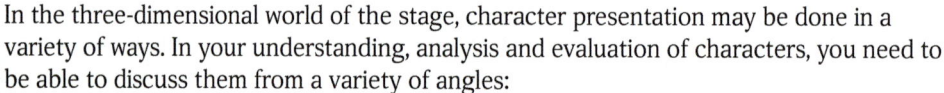

In the three-dimensional world of the stage, character presentation may be done in a variety of ways. In your understanding, analysis and evaluation of characters, you need to be able to discuss them from a variety of angles:

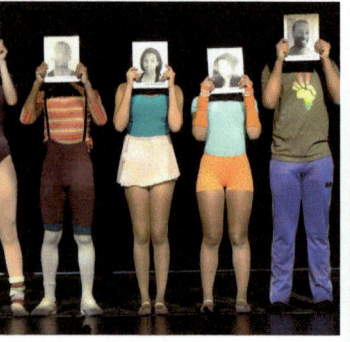

Personal characteristics	What appear to be the character's strengths?	How are these revealed?
	What appear to be the character's weaknesses?	Consider dialogue, actions, soliloquies, costume and stage directions.
	How does the character view the world?	Where in the text is this revealed?
	What motivates the character?	
	How is the character dressed? Does this change at any point? Is this important?	
Relationships with others	With whom is the character close?	How is this revealed?
	With whom is the character in conflict?	Consider dialogue, soliloquies, actions, costume and stage directions.
Development throughout the play	Does the character change over the course of the action?	How is this revealed?
	If so, what are these changes?	Consider dialogue, soliloquies, actions, costume and stage directions.

Check for subtext

As the name implies, subtext is what's going on under the surface of the text. In a good play, this may be what we're really interested in. Perhaps it's not what the character says, but rather what they don't say that's important for the audience's understanding.

How may we detect this subtext?

- **Mismatch of words and body language** – in a seemingly polite conversation, fists may be being clenched, suggesting a relationship is not what it appears on the surface.

- **Mismatch of words and clothes** – the 'socially concerned' character may be wearing designer clothes, suggesting the character's motivation is not what it appears to be.

- **Overdoing protest** – the career woman who behaves hostilely to children may secretly desire to be a mother.

The essential truth of the plot is often revealed by what's going on in the subtext. Be alert to its possibilities for comment.

contd

Textual Analysis: Commenting on drama

What to look out for in staging

In the text	Where does the action take place? In what period does it happen? Over what time scale does the action take place?	How does the author convey this? Consider stage decor, stage props and costumes.
On the stage	What does the stage set reveal about the characters' social/financial situation?	How is this revealed? Consider stage decor, stage props and costumes.

STAGING AND SUBTEXT

The physical placing of characters in relation to each other can say much about a relationship and, therefore, merits your critical attention. A husband and wife at opposite ends of a room when they are trying to resolve marital difficulties says a great deal about whether they're succeeding ... Be alert, too, to how characters gravitate towards or away from each other as they speak. Reconciliation and conflict can be as powerfully articulated by physical movement as by words in the dialogue. These are all aspects of the subtext mentioned earlier.

What to look out for in structure

Exposition – setting the scene	This introduces us to the characters, their social situation and their relationships with each other.
Development – when things start to change	This usually occurs when a new character arrives, or something happens to change the existing situation.
Climax – as a result of growing tension	The development section is usually marked by emerging tensions between the characters, often precipitated by the arrival of the new character or changed circumstances. A crisis or confrontation will painfully sweep away previously held views of people or situations.
Resolution – a changed perspective	As a result of the crisis or confrontation, a new, clearer view of reality emerges. Previous misunderstandings or misconceptions are replaced, however painfully, by much more realistic appreciations of characters and relationships.

What to look out for in themes

A theme is **what the play is about.** A plot is how this theme (or themes) is revealed. The theme will emerge largely through dialogue. As everyday events happen to, and are discussed by, characters, these themes will gradually be revealed.	Is there a political theme? That is, what's being said about the outside world of great events as they affect the circle of our characters?	How is this revealed?
	Is there a social theme? That is, what's being said about the way people interact in, or react to, society around them?	How is this revealed?
	Is there a moral theme? That is, what's being said about the way the characters deal with each other?	How is this revealed?

THINGS TO DO AND THINK ABOUT

Commenting on drama

With a partner, take the first scene of a play which is new to you both. Once you've read it, try to answer the questions posed in the third columns above on character presentation, staging and themes. Highlight quotations to back up your answers. Often, you'll find evidence in more than one quotation or incident.

Does your scene present any evidence of a subtext? A comment on this would really demonstrate your evaluative appreciation of the text.

ONLINE

While the 'How to review a play' link at the Digital Zone focuses on writing a review of a play, rather than answering an exam question on drama, it's still very helpful. Pay attention to the section headed 'Writing the review', particularly the bullet point 'Interpret, Analyze, Evaluate'.

LITERARY STUDY

WHAT ARE YOU BEING ASKED TO DO?

SQA define the literary study element of the Advanced Higher English course as providing an opportunity to 'assess candidates' ability to apply the skills of critical analysis and evaluation to previously studied literary text'.

This will be achieved under exam conditions, where you'll be given the choice of 'one question from a range of questions' and you'll have to 'write a critical essay in response to it'. You'll be able to select this question from poetry, prose fiction, prose non-fiction or drama. You will write this essay under exam conditions in one hour and thirty minutes, and your answer will be awarded a mark out of 20 (20% of the total mark).

It is important that you do NOT choose the texts that you have used in your dissertation.

Initially, you may think to yourself that you've been writing critical literature essays under exam conditions in N5 and Higher, so this shouldn't cause you any problems. But beware – there are some major differences between writing for Advanced Higher and other levels. As with every other aspect of the course, you are 'moving up a gear'.

DON'T FORGET

At Advanced Higher English, the writing of an essay in the *Literary Study* paper is allowing you to crystallise your thoughts about certain aspects of the texts you have chosen to write about. Your mind will be crammed full of information you've read, or heard from your teachers or critics, but **the examiner wants to find out what you think**. While you're trying to answer the question, you're also discovering and developing your own critical views. Having the confidence to do this, and the ability to justify your own views, are some of the key aspects the examiner will be looking for.

THE DIFFERENCES BETWEEN A CRITICAL ESSAY AND A LITERARY STUDY ESSAY

You may think the answer to this question is obvious: I'm being asked to write about a text or texts I have read – or been taught – in answer to a question on the exam paper. Yes, this is true, but there's more to it than that.

At this level, you are not simply unpacking information you've been given by your teacher, or have found in various study guides – this will not constitute a successful essay for the *Literary Study* paper. What you are being asked to do here is to think of the word 'essay' not as a noun, but as a verb.

You are to construct your essay: this means becoming actively involved in what is an intellectual process. If you accept this approach, you'll see that you are actually attempting, trying, testing, trialling your own ideas. You are expressing your own critical thoughts, which have been informed and refined by the views of others. This is the essential difference between writing about literature at this level and other levels.

Key features of successful literary study essays

Although, as we've mentioned, you're 'moving up a gear' to reach this level, the fundamental questions about any work of literature focus on the same two aspects – that is, what the text has to say and how it says it. So, any successful essay in the *Literary Study* paper will communicate a response which shows that you have thought about the ideas in the text and the ways – or techniques – in which these ideas have been conveyed.

THINGS TO DO AND THINK ABOUT

So, what makes a good literature essay?

With a partner, try to list as many features of a critical essay as you can. When you've done this, number them in order of importance and compare your list with the list below.

A good literature essay should:

Answer all aspects of the question
Have a clear structure
Have a strong and clear introduction and conclusion
Illustrate and develop a clear line of independent thought
Convey a sense of personal engagement
Where possible, show originality
Range over the contexts of the texts as opposed to microanalysis
Use relevant quotations effectively, including those from secondary sources
Include an analysis of language
Use advanced critical vocabulary
Be well expressed and accurately written
Be interesting for the examiner
Fulfil the assessment objectives
Be completed in the time allocated

Of course, you may have come up with more – all of which will make a valuable contribution.

ONLINE

Having confidence in your own opinions can sometimes be difficult to achieve. Have a look at the 'What is critical writing' link on the Digital Zone for some interesting and helpful advice.

LITERARY STUDY
DEVELOPING IDEAS AND OPINIONS

SELF-REFLECTION

When you were studying literature at N5 and Higher levels, your teachers will have had a large input into your thinking about the texts you were studying. At these levels, it's sometimes easier just to accept their views, as opposed to attempting to formulate your own and then worrying about justifying them.

At Advanced Higher, you should filter out those views you don't agree with and focus on your own. This may seem easier said than done, but you'll find that the more essays you write about particular texts and authors and the more you discuss topics and views with the other students, the more confident you'll become in your own literary understanding. In fact, by the end of the course you could find yourself re-examining your earlier work and questioning yourself over your views.

You are embarking on a journey of self-discovery. Such self-reflection is a key stage in the process of writing a good literature essay and is, in fact, what makes the writing of such essay an essential part of the course.

STANDING ON YOUR OWN TWO FEET

As we've highlighted before, good literature essays are not all about the ability to show detailed knowledge of a text or texts: they are also about illustrating informed opinions, relevant ideas and your own feelings. If you're prepared to think for yourself; consider and evaluate what other people have written or said; and are not afraid to develop your own critical voice, the experience of studying literature at Advanced Higher level will be a rewarding one. This, like many other aspects of the course, is an invaluable skill for academic study and, perhaps more importantly, life in general.

To succeed, you should guard against taking any short cuts on your journey of self-discovery. While, in the initial stages of the course, modelling can be very useful in that it provides you with an idea of what's required and how to achieve it, later, the heavy reliance of such supports can be like wearing a straight-jacket: you'll lack the freedom to move and develop your own ideas. To do well in your literature essay, you need to have the confidence to stand on your own two feet without any artificial support.

SECRET FORMULA?

You'll probably be familiar with formulas such as SEXY and PEA or PEE for constructing paragraphs in literature essays. You may also have been told to use a 'flagging' structure with topic sentences beginning with 'Firstly', 'Secondly,' etc. While both of these techniques have their place at certain levels, they tend to make the essays read as being rather mechanical.

Here's some more bad news – there is no secret formula.

The good news is, however, writing for Advanced Higher English is, thankfully, not like putting together a piece of flat-

DON'T FORGET

Don't re-invent the wheel. Much of this also applied to the dissertation which you will have written by this time. Remember that the assessment criteria are the same for all the different parts – **knowledge and understanding, analysis, and evaluation**.

contd

packed furniture – there are no set instructions that you must rigidly follow. You have the freedom to express your own views and opinions – within reason. If you want to achieve a good grade, there are certain conventions you should adhere to within that freedom – for example, giving your essay a structure.

 ONLINE

The SQA highlight the importance of **knowledge and understanding, analysis, and evaluation** on page 6 of their 'Course Assessment Specification' document which you'll find at www.brightredbooks.net

 THINGS TO DO AND THINK ABOUT

At this point, it's worth looking at the list you made for what makes a good literature essay and thinking about your dissertation. Make a table like the one below – or use this one – and you will see how many similarities there are.

	LITERATURE ESSAY	DISSERTATION
Answer all aspects of the question/topic		
Have a clear structure		
Have a strong and clear introduction and conclusion		
Illustrate and develop a clear line of independent thought		
Convey a sense of personal engagement		
Where possible, show originality		
Range of the contexts of the texts as opposed to microanalysis		
Use relevant quotations effectively		
Include an analysis of language		
Use advanced critical vocabulary		
Be well expressed and accurately written		
Be interesting for the examiner		
Fulfil the assessment criteria		
Be completed in the time allocated		

Now, using the table below, make a list of the main differences between a good essay for the *Literary Study* paper and a dissertation. Hopefully, you will find that there are more similarities than differences.

	LITERATURE ESSAY	DISSERTATION

Discuss your findings with a partner.

LITERARY STUDY

DISSECTING THE QUESTIONS

THE QUESTIONS

In the *Literary Study* exam, there will be various types of questions. Although these different types will require slightly different approaches, their aims are the same – to allow you to show your knowledge and understanding and your ability to analyse and evaluate the texts you've chosen to write about.

In comparison with N5 and Higher, the questions are very open – they're inviting you to discuss the issues, and they're encouraging you to develop personal judgements about the texts. It is this that the examiner will be interested in seeing.

TYPES OF QUESTIONS

As you did at N5 and Higher, the most effective way to prepare for this part of the course is to be fully aware of the kinds of questions you might be asked and to know what they're asking you to do. If you look at past papers, you'll notice that there are a number of verbs that SQA use in their *Literary Study* paper. The main ones are 'discuss', 'analyse', 'compare', 'evaluate', and wording such as 'to what extent'. However, there are others which may appear in the future such as 'explore', 'explain' and 'examine'. What exactly are these words telling you about the way in which you should answer the question?

Let's have a look at some specific question types.

Discuss

For example:

> Discuss how internal and external conflict is central to the dramatic impact of any two plays.

Here, the use of 'discuss' is suggesting that different people may have different views – discussion of a single view would therefore be self-limiting. In this type of question, you could also include any critical evaluation of the ideas themselves. This, of course, would add weight to your personal response.

Also, notice in this question the use of the word 'how'. Although a very small word, it's a very important one. But, what does it mean in terms of answering the question? It means that you should focus on the techniques that the respective playwrights have used to convey the internal and external conflict.

Analyse

For example:

> Analyse the effectiveness of the treatment of love in any of its forms (romantic, erotic, maternal, paternal …) in three poems.

While it's assumed that most questions in the *Literary Study* paper will require you to include some form of analysis, when it is highlighted in the question, you'll be required to examine, in detail, specific stylistic techniques used by the writer. In this question, you would focus closely on how the poet or poets have used language to create particular effects. If this type of question appeared in the drama section, you would focus on dramatic techniques.

contd

Compare

For example:

> Compare and contrast the treatment of love in any two novels.

This type of question will be new to you. Normally, it deals with texts which are linked by a theme, and so, the key focus should be on the way in which the particular theme is presented and developed. Like most questions, this requires an analytical approach, but it also needs to incorporate comparisons and contrasts. The thing to avoid with this type of question – as in the dissertation – is writing about the texts separately – you need to adopt an integrated approach to the comparisons or contrasts.

Evaluate and discuss to what extent

For example:

> 'The aim for the writer – journalist, travel writer, diarist, commentator, biographer – is to encourage the reader to reflect, inquire and to be inspired.'
>
> Discuss to what extent at least two non-fiction texts have succeeded in achieving one or more of these responses from the reader.

The use of phrases such 'evaluate' and 'to what extent' imply that there is more than one view or opinion. As a result, you'll be able to agree or disagree with the critical position in the question. You must not be daunted by this. You are entitled to your opinion – if you can justify it with references from the texts.

Remember, the ability to present an effective counter argument is an important indicator within the assessment criteria. Where the question contains a proposition – such as this one – a criticism often made by examiners is that students simply mention it and then move on to write about something else. Always take the proposition into account and use it as the basis for your response.

 DON'T FORGET

The key thing in all of this is that you **read the question carefully**, select the **keywords**, and write about what you have been asked.

APPROACHING QUESTIONS

When you meet any question you've not seen before, it's extremely important that you read it carefully and spend time thinking about what you are being asked to write about. Sometimes, you could see a question – perhaps similar to one you've practised – and not realise that it's slightly different. You would then be writing what you wanted to write and not what the question was asking.

A useful way to make sure that you read the question carefully is to circle, underline or highlight keywords, and then note down, very briefly, what the question is asking you to do.

For example:

> (Discuss) the use of (satire) and (mockery) to (expose) the (weakness) of (humanity) in any (three) poems.

ONLINE

When an element of an exam is relatively new, it can be difficult to find previous questions to practise with. However, other exam boards also provide closed-book exam questions. Follow the link on the Digital Zone to find some examples.

 THINGS TO DO AND THINK ABOUT

Look at a selection of past *Literary Study* questions. Read them carefully and select the keywords from each question. Think about what the focus of each of the keywords is. You may find it useful to work with a partner and discuss your ideas.

When you have a 'feel' for the type of questions you will be asked, choose two of the texts you've been studying. Make up three different types of questions on these texts. Swap with your partner and discuss the focus of each question.

LITERARY STUDY
CONSTRUCTING THE ESSAY

DEVELOPING A LINE OF THOUGHT

Now that you've dissected the question and have a good idea of what's being asked, you will start to plan and structure your answer. Although you've been doing this now for several years, the major difference at this level is that it's very important to establish and then develop a line of thought which will run through your answer.

So, before you launch into your 'grand plan', write down the keywords from the question and your key points. Then stop and think.

- Are the points you've written down arranged in a logical progression of thought?
- After your introduction, write about your strongest point next – which one is that?
- Which one should you write about next?
- Will you be able to link these successfully?

Making connections

This is an exam, so time is of the essence. There several ways in which you can convince your examiner that you have carefully considered the question and are developing a line of thought in light of it.

One way is to use the keywords from the question. You will have done this before, so you will also be aware that the overuse of these words can make the essay seem rather mechanical and lacking vitality. However, in the initial stages of writing essays at this level, using them – in moderation – can be extremely helpful.

Another way is to have a bank of connectives which you can dip into. Phrases such as 'however', 'moreover' and 'additionally', are ones you will have used before. Now think about including phrases such as 'the most significant', 'the most powerful' and 'the most effective'. By employing these kinds of words and phrases, you're creating the impression that you have considered a number of views or examples and have chosen this particular one because it best illustrates your line of thought.

In an ideal world, you'll have gone through the process of evaluation to arrive at your most effective example, but even if you haven't, using these words and phrases will create the impression that you have. The creation of a sense of evaluation and self-reflection is essential at this level.

A more 'sophisticated', but slightly more difficult way – in an exam – to connect your paragraphs is to make sure that the last sentence of a paragraph provides a hint or – if you are better organised – an indication, of the subject of the next paragraph.

DON'T FORGET

Too often, candidates assume that the links they make as their line of thought develops are obvious. Yes, they may be to you, but not always to the examiner. Examiners cannot see into your head. Make the links clear.

 ACTIVITY

Although many students feel that they have critically assessed their own work, this is a very difficult thing to do. Here's a method which you could find useful.

Take a blank sheet of paper and write down the keywords from the question at the top. Underneath, write down the line of thought you want to develop in your response: this will be the basis of your introduction. By establishing this early, you'll be able to constantly refer back to it, and this will help your examiner follow your thought process.

Now, list the points you want to make, leaving spaces between them. Have you listed them in order of importance? If you have – fine. If you have not, reorder them. Now focus on how you're going to link the paragraphs. Insert words or phrases between the points. Are you using the same words too often? Are you jumping about? Does what you've written illustrate structural strength and logic?

USING SIGNPOSTS

You have now started on your journey: you have planned your route and you know where your destination is. All you have to do now is follow the planned route. Well, unfortunately, it's not always that simple.

From time to time on journeys, we notice another route, one which looks more interesting, and turn off! Hopefully we're still heading in the same direction, but using minor as opposed to major roads. Sometimes, we're diverted onto other roads because of accidents, or sometimes the sat nav doesn't work properly and we get lost! You don't want such things to happen on your literary journey.

If, by any chance, you do take your examiner off your planned route, you must clearly signpost that you are doing so and why. Then, the examiner will be able to follow where you're taking them, appreciate the detour, then smoothly re-join the original route. For example, if you are including a counterargument to what you've been writing about, make sure the examiner doesn't think that you've started to travel in the opposite direction. If you don't signpost, you'll look like you're contradicting yourself.

Consider the following:

The text chosen is *The Master of Ballantrae* by Robert Louis Stevenson and there is a discussion of the main character James Durie. James is, in many ways, the complete opposite of his brother Henry, and so a discussion of Henry would highlight different aspects of James's character. For example:

Paragraph 1

> In *The Master of Ballantrae*, James Durie is a dashing, roguish character who fights alongside Prince Charlie in the Battle of Culloden. This essay explores these aspects of James's character, supported with effective textual quotations.

Paragraph 2

> James is cruel and malicious, while Henry is dull and ordinary. This essay goes on to illustrate the contrast between James and Henry.

Providing clear signposting here would avoid what could appear a contradiction. Very simply, the word 'however' could have been added at the beginning of the topic sentence of the second paragraph, but it would be clearer if the contradictory facets of James's character were highlighted.

The second paragraph could start with a topic sentence:

> Although James could initially appear as a dashing and roguish character, beneath this charisma he is cruel and malicious.

 **DON'T FORGET**

Poor, or no, signposting will make reading your essay a frustrating experience for the examiner.

 ONLINE

More detail is provided in the section on 'Academic Writing and Style' at www.brightredbooks.net

 ## THINGS TO DO AND THINK ABOUT

A way to check if you're developing your line of thought, and including clear signposting, is to take the sheet of paper you used in the *Activity*, and cut it up into separate paragraphs.

Mix them up and give them to a partner asking him or her to arrange them in a logical order. If your partner finds the task really difficult, perhaps your line of thought and signposting aren't clear enough. Discuss what happens.

Remember, criticism should always be constructive.

LITERARY STUDY

STRUCTURING ESSAYS ON MORE THAN ONE TEXT

The questions in the *Literary Study* exam paper ask you to write about more than one text. Although this is what you've been doing in your dissertation, it's not something you have done before under exam conditions.

Before you can really come to terms with writing about two or more texts, **you must know your texts well**. It's only when you have a good knowledge of them that you'll be able to make connections between them. This is clearly more complex than just writing about a single text. Sometimes, under pressure in the exam, it might seem easier to write about one text and then the other, perhaps attempting to link them in the conclusion. But essays written in this way are not usually awarded high marks.

DEVELOPING AN APPROACH

The most important step in this process is the planning and, after that, thinking about the time you have. It's a good idea to consider spending quite a lot of your time making notes – jotting down ideas for making connections, linking, signposting, paragraph planning – and thinking; and leaving less of the time to actually write your essay. Initially this could appear too little time for the latter but, remember the adage 'quality not quantity'.

The next step is to find a substantial link between the texts. You could be lucky enough to be given the link in the question – for example, 'Compare and contrast three poetic treatments of the theme of loss'. Or, you may have to find it for yourself – 'Discuss some of the principal means by which tension is created and sustained in any two novels'. Obviously, the second question here is more challenging.

Regardless of which type of question you choose to answer, your starting point is to find a substantial link. The word 'substantial' is important because, if there's not enough overlap or contrast between the texts, it will be difficult to sustain a connection. You must watch, however, that there is not too much overlap, because then your discussion could become heavily weighted towards one text.

Let's look closely at these examples.

Example 1

Example 2

Example 3

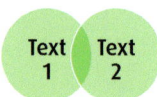

Example 1 indicates that there are not enough connections between the texts. If you have made notes beforehand, you should not find yourself in this situation.

Example 2 indicates that there is too much overlap. In other words, you have one text which you can write about in far more detail than the other. Again, your notes should help you to avoid this situation.

Example 3 is an illustration of what you should be aiming for. Here, there are enough connections between the two texts to allow you to discuss both in adequate detail.

DON'T FORGET

When writing about more than one text, it's essential to discuss them together.

Literary Study: Structuring essays on more than one text

 THINGS TO DO AND THINK ABOUT

Consider the effectiveness of the following basic structures. When you are doing so, remember to look at the Venn diagrams above.

Example 1:
Introduction
Text 1 – Main Point
Text 1 – Secondary Point
Text 2 – Main Point
Text 2 – Secondary Point
Conclusion

Example 2:
Introduction
Text 1 – Main Point
Text 1 – Secondary point
Text 2 – Main Point
Text 2 – Secondary Point
Texts 1 and 2 – Comparisons of Main Points
Texts 1 and 2 – Comparisons of Secondary Points
Conclusion

Example 3:
Introduction
Texts 1 and 2 – Main Points
Texts 1 and 2 – Secondary Points
Texts 1 and 2 – Tertiary Points
Conclusion
Commentary

Hopefully you would reject Example 1 because it is writing about one text followed by the other, with little or no attempt to make connections between the two. The second example is slightly better in that there is an attempt to compare the two texts – although this is done at the end. Example 3 is the one you should be aiming for, because it's making connections between the texts under topic headings.

Remember, achieving this will only come with practice.

Now, think about the perfect question for two of the texts you've been studying. Imagine that you are going to answer this question. Then, draw up a plan – hopefully using Example 3 above. Of course, this is a basic plan and you will have to fill in more detail.

LITERARY STUDY

WRITING ABOUT MORE THAN ONE POEM

WHAT TO EXPECT IN THE EXAM

It's extremely unlikely that you'll be asked to write about only one poem in the exam. You will have studied a collection of poems, either by a single poet or several different poets, so you could be asked to write about three or more poems.

Questions are relatively general, therefore, it's a good idea to decide in advance which poems you would want to discuss in detail, perhaps briefly referring to others.

But how do you organise your writing on a collection of poems?

STRATEGIES FOR COMPARING AND CONTRASTING POEMS

	POEM 1	POEM 2
Subject		
Theme		
Speaker		
Situation		
Form or structure		
Rhyme and rhythm		
Tone		
Atmosphere		
Mood		
Imagery		
Vocabulary		
Figures of speech		
Relevant biographical information		

The way most students would tackle this is to take the two or three poems which they have chosen and work through them, analysing them in sequence. There's nothing wrong with this approach, if it is only the initial stage of this process. If you adopt a poem-by-poem approach, it's difficult to make connections across the poems. What this could lead to is an answer structured as either Example 1 or Example 2 on the previous page.

A more effective technique is to think of the poems as a group, and explore the connections. In order to do this, it's useful to have some kind of framework which will help you to structure your thoughts and, subsequently, your answer.

To the left is an example you could use or adapt:

Clearly, this is a basic framework and all the headings may not apply to the poems you have chosen. When comparing poems in this way, you would need to complete a much deeper analysis and you will want to add to this as you revise and practise questions.

Below is a possible comparison of the poems 'Hawk in the Rain' and 'Hawk Roosting' by Ted Hughes. *NOTE: it has not been fully completed in case you want to use this example – it is important to develop your own interpretations.*

	POEM 1 – 'HAWK IN THE RAIN'	POEM 2 – 'HAWK ROOSTING'
Subject	Hawk and Man	Hawk
Theme	Superiority of animals over man – inability to understand death. Man's world is ever changing.	Again, Man as a lesser being. Hawk's world is timeless and permanent. Same theme but refined.
Speaker	Hughes himself – one voice.	As if the hawk has consented to an interview. He has two voices – one that drafts out his view of the world and his purpose, 'I am going to keep things like this', and a second that knows man will be unable to understand his view – he has 'no falsifying dream', 'no sophistry'.
Situation	Hughes compares himself to the hawk – master of all he surveys – defies natural laws – but Hughes is struggling with the elements, trying unsuccessfully to defy them. Hughes inhabits a world of choices and where things are always changing.	Hawk has no natural enemies and has secured his position – 'through the allotment of death'. He inhabits a world with no choices and where things never change.
Form or structure	First in anthology – indication of the style of later poems.	Monologue. Cyclical – begins and ends with 'I' – nothing will change. Regular length to stanzas – hawk – tight control of situation.

contd

Literary Study: Writing about more than one poem

Rhyme and rhythm	Free verse	Free verse
		Irregular metre – hawk above such things.
Tone		Menacing, sinister, confident
Atmosphere	Depressing	
Mood	Hawk is not afraid of death	
Imagery	Vivid imagery – look at description of hawk.	Hawk is a like a God – he is the perfect killing machine. He determines the fate of others – 'to tear off heads'.
		Chilling imagery – 'nothing will change'.
Vocabulary	Predominance of verbs, for example, 'Thumbs my eyes, throws my breath, tackles my heart and rain hacks my head to the bone …'	Direct and abrupt language.
		Violent – 'tear off heads'.
		Repetition of negatives 'nothing has changed'.
Figures of speech	Alliteration – throughout – letter 'd' – 'I drowned in the drumming ploughland' and 'I drag up'.	Assonance – 'feet', 'sleep', 'eat', 'tree' – screech of the hawk.
	Letter 'm' – 'Smashed, mix his heart's blood with the mire of the land'.	
	Simile – 'steady as a hallucination'.	
	Metaphor – 'morsel in the earth's mouth'.	
	Personification – 'clutching clay'.	
Relevant biographical information	Yorkshire – fascination with animals from an early age.	Hughes stated that the poem was about a Hawk – not a dictator.

By analysing the poems in this way, the following main points emerge:

Similarities

	POEM 1 – 'HAWK IN THE RAIN'	POEM 2 – 'HAWK ROOSTING'
Subject	Hawk – centre of nature's power – natural forces.	Hawk centre – but a bloody world.
Language	Concise, straightforward, powerful.	Concise, straightforward, violent.

Differences

	POEM 1 – 'HAWK IN THE RAIN'	POEM 2 – 'HAWK ROOSTING'
Perspective	Use of 'I' – human being.	Use of 'I' – hawk.
Plot	Story of a hawk who witnesses a human being's fragility.	No plot development – hawk enjoys his static situation.

THINGS TO DO AND THINK ABOUT

Take two, or even three, poems that you've been studying. Try to complete a comparison table for them. By doing this exercise, you will become aware of just how much time it takes. However, it is an extremely useful way to organise your revision.

DON'T FORGET

You will not have time to produce this type of detailed analysis in the exam, but using something like this should help you to arrange your thoughts for your revision programme, as well as your thoughts before you start writing in the exam.

ONLINE

Ted Hughes was a famous poet and there are numerous articles which have been written about his poetry. To find out more, have a look at the link on the Digital Zone.

LITERARY STUDY

WRITING ABOUT MORE THAN ONE NOVEL

WRITING ABOUT LONGER TEXTS

While when you are tackling questions about poetry, you could be writing about three or more poems; when you are tackling questions about novels, you'll probably only be writing about two or three novels. Initially, the task of writing about two long texts could seem daunting. But, don't let it be.

Novels also come in many forms and the best place to start is using the same principles as you would for poetry – identify what they are about and try to establish some comparisons. What are the broad connections? Is there a common theme? Are there any similarities in style?

However, what you must take into consideration when writing about novels is that there are, in the main, two ways of thinking about them – the novel as a 'world' created by the author, and the novel as a creative work.

If you think of the novel as a 'world' created by the author, what is important to you is the content. Hopefully, you will have been able to become part of this 'world' – interacting with the people, places, events, etc. If you can do this, you'll be able to write about the characters and events as if they really did happen or could happen.

If you think about the novel as a work of art, you will adopt a far more objective view about what you have been reading. You will approach it from a more analytical perspective. This time you'll think about the characters and events as devices the author has created to convey a theme or message. When adopting this type of approach, the language the writer has used will be of prime importance.

STRATEGIES FOR COMPARING AND CONTRASTING TWO NOVELS

When you are thinking about longer texts, you must be familiar with them so that you can 'work them' – that is, you must be able to locate incidents and important parts of the novels quickly. You may find it useful to annotate your texts, or use different coloured inserts, to help you with this. Start simple – don't rush into making detailed comparisons. You can focus on that later when you begin to practise different types of questions.

You might find the following table useful:

	NOVEL 1 *NORTHANGER ABBEY*	**NOVEL 2 *WUTHERING HEIGHTS***
Genre	Parody of the Gothic and sentimental romance novel.	Gothic romance.
Narrative viewpoint	Third-person narrator – limited – Catherine's decisions are often wrong and flawed. The intrusive narrator – 'my heroine' – following conventions of the genres.	Lockwood is the main narrator, but other characters, such as Nelly, are an influence. Not a limited viewpoint – can understand events from the point of view of other characters.
Structure	Two volumes – relatively well balanced. Volume one – parody of the sentimental romance. Volume two – parody of the Gothic.	Not chronological – use of flashbacks – highlights the influence of the past on the present and connects the fate of Catherine and Heathcliff. Flashback 1 – Catherine's diary is read by Lockwood. Flashback 2 – Heathcliff's arrival. Flashback 3 – Hareton is born.

contd

Literary Study: Writing about more than one novel

Setting	Volume one – Bath – busy city relatively modern. Volume two – Northanger Abbey – ancient.	Wild, desolate Yorkshire moors – the houses of Wuthering Heights and Thrushcross Grange.
Main female characters	Heroine – Catherine Morland – protagonist. Eleanor Tilney, Isabella Thorpe – antagonists.	Heroine – Catherine Earnshaw – protagonist. Isabella – antagonist.
Main male characters	Hero – Henry Tilney – protagonist. General Tilney, John Thorpe – antagonists.	Hero – Heathcliff – protagonist. Hindley Earnshaw – antagonist.
Other characters	Mr and Mrs Allen, Mrs Thorpe	Edgar Linton, Catherine Linton, Hareton Earnshaw, Linton Heathcliff, Lockwood, Nelly Dean
Climax	General Tilney sends Catherine home.	Catherine's death.
Themes	Education – Catherine needs to be educated and socialised – importance of reading to this. Imagination and common sense – initially Catherine lacks imagination like her mother and then she develops a vivid imagination.	Love – passionate love between Catherine and Heathcliff – but it is a destructive love. Revenge – Heathcliff's overwhelming desire for this, but Hindley sees Heathcliff usurping his position. Death and the supernatural – Catherine and Heathcliff.
Use of language	Narrative voice moves in and out of the consciousness of the characters. Lack of vivid descriptive writing. Consider hyperbole especially.	Different types of language used according to character – for example: Lockwood – educated, Nelly – colloquial, Heathcliff – passionate. Focus on vivid description.
Symbols	Northanger Abbey	Moors, ghosts, weather, gates and doors.
Social, political, historical and/or cultural background	Written in 1798–99, a period of social and political turmoil in England – Habeas Corpus, influence of the French Revolution, people were beginning to be judged by the goods they owned, rising demand for novels.	Victorian attitude to morals, romance and nature.

 **DON'T FORGET**

Although the genre is different, and perhaps the way you tackle it is different, you will still be focusing on the relationship between the ideas the writers are conveying and how they are conveying them.

If you have time, as with all the genres, doing some research on the authors and the time in which they are writing could be useful. If you know something about the social, political and/or cultural background of the time, this could help you to understand aspects which may initially be puzzling – for example, with the novels above, the background to the Gothic and sentimental romance novels and the attitudes prevalent in Victorian society.

 THINGS TO DO AND THINK ABOUT

Draw up a similar table for two novels you have studied. Remember to focus on the main aspects and use your annotated or marked extracts to illustrate these.

LITERARY STUDY

WRITING ABOUT MORE THAN ONE PLAY

THE DIFFERENCE BETWEEN DRAMA AND OTHER GENRES

Drama can sometimes be quite tricky to write about because you're writing about something which was written to be performed and seen. Plays may seem very quick and easy to read in comparison with other genres, but this relative lack of detail can lead to problems when writing a literature essay at this level.

A play is essentially a drama script which focuses on dialogue and stage directions. Such a genre cannot provide the wealth of detail in terms of description and characterisation that prose can, nor can it provide the vivid imagery of poetry. However, plays do convey meaningful themes.

There are other aspects of drama which need to be taken into consideration. For example, sometimes it's very important that a character is on stage even if he or she may not be speaking. How are you to assess the effect of this? How do the audience react to them? Such situations lead to personal interpretation.

While it must be acknowledged that some playwrights such as Tennessee Williams wrote very detailed stage directions, including instructions for lighting and the colour of costumes, this is not the norm. If you want to successfully write a literature essay on a play, it's important to see it in production. You may not have easy access to the theatre, but sometimes there are films of productions or clips on the internet. Through actually watching a play, in any medium, you'll be able to appreciate the possibilities afforded by stage setting, lighting, costumes, etc.

STRATEGIES FOR COMPARING AND CONTRASTING TWO PLAYS

So, what do you need to be aware of when writing about drama?

At a basic level, it's the same as prose – setting, characterisation, plot and theme. However, due to the differences between the genres, you need to be aware of other aspects – some of which are more difficult to grasp. It's therefore important that you take notes on them before you start writing. Try to focus on the main points or aspects that make a particular play different from the others you have studied.

You might find the following table useful. Here, we compare Anton Chekhov's play's *The Cherry Orchard* and *Uncle Vanya*. NOTE: it has not been fully completed in case you want to use this example – it is important to develop your own interpretations.

	PLAY 1 *THE CHERRY ORCHARD*	PLAY 2 *UNCLE VANYA*
Theme	Memory. Modernism and old Russia.	Monotony of characters' lives, impossible love.
Dramatic style – classical, natural, modern, natural absurd	Psychological naturalism.	Realism.
Genre – tragedy, comedy	Tragicomedy.	Tragicomedy.
Structure – plot, acts, scene changes	Tightly unified by Lyuba and the sale of the cherry orchard. Act 1 – introducing characters Act 2 – rising action Act 3 – climax of sale	Unconventional plot construction – concentric action – illustrates how individuals survive and live in considerable suffering.

contd

Literary Study: Writing about more than one play

Setting – time, place	Real world in which the characters exist, and the representative world of the stage. Country estate – 'nursery'. May through to October. Setting has symbolic meaning and relevance. Orchard – associated with the past, the present and the future – symbol of a better life ahead.	Serebryakov's country estate. Setting has symbolic meaning and relevance. Twenty-six roomed house – described as a 'morgue' and as if it had 'fallen from the earth onto some foreign planet'. External setting reflects internal action.
Protagonist	Ranyevskaya	Donetsk, Sonya, Vanya, Yelena
Antagonist	Lopakhin	Serebryakov
Secondary characters	Important on the social level – how they react to social change.	Telegin – different because he seems contented.
Stage directions – set, lighting, props, costumes	Lighting, fake snow, etc., End – in the silence which follows 'a distant sound is heard, as if the sky, the sound of breaking string dying away, mournful'.	Important in the description of the house – 'no curtains' 'no pictures'. Lack of any specific detail regarding time. Costumes of the period.
Language – dialogue, accent	Comic in places – Act 1 – 'Would you care to take your pills now?'. Charlotta's monologue in Act 2. Lopakhin's bleating.	Realistic – reflects the socio-economic status of the characters, for example, Marina the maid. Soliloquies – convey a sense of urgency, for example, 'I've become a different man …' Act 1, and 'Ivan Petronivich, you are an educated man…'
Symbolism/motif	Weather – discussed a great deal – underlines the shallowness of the relationships. Trees – orchard – past coming under threat – in the end, trees cut down.	Weather – Astrov – 'It's so close today'. 'Storm brewing outside'. Trees – symbolic significance of the destruction and replanting. Lacking symbols in comparison with *The Cherry Orchard*.
Atmosphere	Isolation and confinement – country house and estate – 'provincial dullness'. Characters explore themselves because of this. Reflective and yearning moods.	Desolation and futility. Melancholic.
Audience reaction		
Context – social, historical, political	Background of change and upheaval in Russian society – post 1861. First play in which there is an awareness of the world outside Russia – people travel by train, Ranyevskaya has just returned from Paris at the beginning of the play. Expands landowners' financial problems and draws on characters from other social classes – Ranyevskaya, Lopakhin, and Trenimon.	Some insight into the landed gentry and the problems which they have making their estates pay, but one-dimensional view of the class system. Play about change, but not social or political change.

As with poetry and prose, not all of these will be applicable to all of the questions you could be faced with, but this forms a basis from which you can work. You can always add in information if you think you might need it.

 THINGS TO DO AND THINK ABOUT

Draw up a similar table for two drama texts you have studied. Remember to focus on aspects with which you are perhaps not as familiar, for example, stage directions and atmosphere.

 **DON'T FORGET**

When you tackle preparation for a literature essay on a play, it's important to realise that the script is only a skeleton and there's a lot more to it than that. It's the inclusion of additional factors that convey a sense of the drama to be seen and heard which will make a difference to your mark.

LITERARY STUDY
TOP TIPS FOR REVISION

DON'T FORGET
Despite what you may think, no one really understands or completely knows a text 'inside out', but multiple readings will help.

READING AND RE-READING YOUR TEXTS

By the time you reach the exam, hopefully, you will feel that you know your texts well. However, reading and re-reading prior to the exam is absolutely vital.

Perhaps you read your texts quite quickly before you started to study them in detail. You might then have focused on specific parts of them. Therefore, it's essential to re-read the whole of your texts, not only to refresh your memory in terms of the plot etc., but also to pick up details you may have forgotten or missed. Clearly, the texts your teacher will have chosen for you to study at this level will be complex, so, every time you read them, you will notice something new. This is part of the process of understanding, not just knowing, your text. And this takes time.

DON'T FORGET
If you feel you know a text well, do not skim over revising it – it may be the text you end up writing about in the exam.

MANAGING YOUR TIME BEFORE THE EXAM

As you already know, time is crucial in exams, but – at this level – time is crucial for revision. You'll not only have to read and re-read your texts, you'll also have to allow sufficient time to prepare, plan and practise a variety of different types of questions. It is also important to keep a balance between the different texts you have studied.

DON'T FORGET
Remember, examiners can spot answers to previous exam questions which have been 'tweaked' to fit another one! Always respond to the exact question that you have been asked, employing your own ideas and opinions.

PREVIOUS EXAM QUESTIONS

As part of your revision, you should try to look at as many past-paper questions as possible. This is important because it will give you a 'feel' or 'flavour' of the types of questions you could be asked. You will also become familiar with the wording and phrasing in the questions. Always remember that, although a question has been asked in the past, there's no guarantee it will not appear again in the future. So, be prepared to think on your feet.

DON'T FORGET
It is extremely important to get as much practice as possible under timed conditions. The more you practise, the quicker you'll get and the more you'll write.

TIMED ESSAYS

A major worry for most people in an exam is, 'will I finish?'. This is only natural and can be a particular worry at this level. In many cases, students run out of time, or rush their conclusions because they've not 'timed' their plan.

If you've spent adequate time planning, you'll know what you want to write. Try inserting some sort of marker into your plan to indicate where you expect to be half way through the time you've allocated to write the essay. By doing this, you'll know where you should be, and you won't be tempted to spend too long on the initial paragraphs of your essay.

You will have practised writing essays in class under timed conditions, but there's no reason why you couldn't repeat the exercise at home – and you will have the benefit of your teacher's feedback.

WRITING YOUR ESSAY IN THE EXAM

Now that you've completed your revision, you should be well prepared to write your essay. Here are some points to keep in mind.

- Read the question carefully. Highlight or write down the keywords.

- Plan your essay.

- In your introduction, you should address the question. It can be useful to repeat the wording of the question, as well as name the texts you're going to write about. You can then follow this with a general indication of your response to the question with a summary of what line of thought you intend to follow. If the question requires it, you can state your viewpoint. In this way, you'll be signposting how your essay will be structured. Remember to keep your introduction brief.

- Always assume that your examiner has read the texts – there's no need to include summaries.

- If you really want to capture your examiner's attention, you could start your essay with a strong viewpoint or quotation and then launch straight into a discussion of the points you have to support your view.

- Develop all of your points clearly, using evidence to support them. Your quotations should be relevant and short. Remember to embed them in your essay and use them to help with your analysis. If you focus on what the writers are saying and how they are saying it, you're more likely to achieve a high mark.

- Make sure that your answer deals with all aspects of the question – effective planning should help you with this.

- Your essay should show a good standard of writing – accurate expression, correct punctuation, grammar and spelling. Always keep in mind that technical accuracy is an aid to effective communication. We can all make mistakes, especially in exams, but these should be few and far between.

- You should be familiar with more literary terms than you realise. You should now be able to incorporate them into your writing with confidence. You will not receive credit for simply knowing them; you must use them appropriately.

- Examiners do not award high marks based on length: they award marks on the basis of what you have achieved. While it's frequently the case that shorter essays do not illustrate sufficient depth of understanding, analysis and evaluation, it's also true that some longer essays can be rambling and lack a clear structure. If you have planned effectively, you should avoid such scenarios.

- Make sure that your essay has a conclusion – and does not just stop. You don't want it to be a repeat of the introduction or the wording of the question. Your conclusion should sum up your ideas. Some students like to end with a relevant and effective quotation, whereas others retain some strong opinion that has been developed elsewhere in the essay. However you decide to conclude, do it with confidence and make sure that your examiner knows your final opinion and you will convey a sense of completeness.

- If you have time, give your essay a title: this will help the examiner to focus on the texts and/or topic you have chosen to write about.

 ONLINE

Follow the link on the Digital Zone to a very useful website, where the section on 'Guidelines for Essay Writing' is particularly relevant to all that has been described.

 THINGS TO DO AND THINK ABOUT

Spend time preparing. Know your texts well. Think about your texts and what they mean to you. Do not leave anything to the last minute. Hopefully, you will now have every chance of achieving success in this part of the course.

FINAL EDITING PROCESS

DISSERTATION AND PORTFOLIO

It may come as a surprise to some, but examiners are only human. In the white heat of the exam room, they accept that technical slips of expression will happen, no matter how rigorous you try to be. However, when it comes to your dissertation and portfolio, their attitude toughens.

You have had, they argue, many months to research and write three texts – significant milestones in your academic career. There can be no excuse now for structural weaknesses, disconnected paragraphs, clumsy sentence structure, tired vocabulary, grammar mistakes, misspellings, or even typos. They are looking for the highest standards of academic expression. Failure to deliver at this level is serious.

Given the effort you've been making to articulate complicated thoughts on various works of literature, and to compose portfolio pieces of originality and depth, you cannot afford to undermine all this work with errors that could be avoided by a thorough editing process. So, how might you set about this?

METHODOLOGY

Leave time

Keep to a sensible work timetable for your dissertation and portfolio and you'll have the time necessary for reflecting fully over the vital final editing process. Let a good few days pass before you even think of going over your 'finished' work again. You will come back to it with fresh eyes, and you'll be astonished by just how many fairly superficial slips you'll find.

Print out the text

It's always easier to proofread with the printed text in front of you. And a red pen in your hand.

Read aloud

Reading your text through silently is not ideal. We tend to 'read' what we think we see rather than what's actually on the page in front of us. Reading aloud reduces this risk. Furthermore, any clumsy sentence structure will emerge as you stumble over its tortured cadences. So, too, will statements that do not quite make sense. Mark a red cross where you stumbled and go back to the awkward corner later.

Involve a partner

Better still than reading aloud to yourself is getting a partner to read your text out to you. They are perhaps even more likely to read what's actually there and not what you think is there. Do they at times fail to follow the logic of your arguments and paragraph sequence? Are there any raised eyebrows?

What made perfect sense to you might not be as transparent to someone else. This might give you valuable insight into any flaws of argument, expression or structure that you haven't noticed before now. (You can return the favour by offering to read theirs!)

ONLINE

For a review of all that we've talked about here regarding correct practice in text creation, check out the 'Purdue Online Writing Lab' link on the Digital Zone.

INDEX

analysis 6–7
  see also devices; mood; tone; word choice
argumentative writing 56–57
author's attitude 6

bibliography 15, 38–39

characterisation 42–43
  drama 52–53
  prose fiction 68
course components see dissertation; literary study; portfolio; revision; textual analysis
critical analysis 7, 34

devices 6–7
dissertation 4, 5, 10–39
  content 10
  final editing 92–95
  planning 8, 12–13, 20–21
  presentation style 11
  research 10
  sources 10
  structure 22–23
    comparative element 22
    conclusion 30–33
    connections 22–23
    contrasts 23
    introduction 22, 26–29, 32–33
    linkage 24–25
  timescale 11
  word limits 10, 20
  writing 34–37
  see also bibliography; footnotes; title; topic; writing
drama 27, 29, 52–55, 88–89

essay 10
  construction 80–81
  critical and literary 74–75
  persuasive 48–49
  reflective 46–47
  structure 82–83
  see also dissertation; writing
evaluation 7

final editing 92–95
footnotes 39
formal tone/style 34–35

genre 8, 40, 58

literary study 4, 5, 9, 74–91
  critical and literary essay 74–75
  developing ideas and opinions 76–77
  dissecting the questions 78–79
  essay construction 80–81

mood 7
motifs 45

notes
  colour coding 14
  evidence 14
  plagiarism 15
  summarising 15
  taking 11, 14–17
  novel 28, 29

objective tone/style 34

persuasive writing 48–49
plotting 44
poetry 28, 29
  textual analysis 60–61, 84–85
portfolio 4, 5, 8–9, 40–57
  argumentative 56–57
  drama 52–55
  final editing 92–95
  persuasive 48–49
  poetry 50–51
  prose fiction 42–45
  reflective 46–47
primary sources 10, 11, 14, 24, 38

reading 12–13
reflective writing 46–47
revision 90–91
rhythm 9

secondary sources 10, 11, 15, 24, 38
setting 43–44
sound 9
speaker identity 6
symbolism 44–45

taking notes see notes, taking
techniques 6–7
textual analysis 4, 5, 9, 58–73
  commenting on poetry 60–61
  drama 72–73
  formal structures 62–65
    rhythm and rhyme 64–65
    stress patterns 63
  free verse and cohesion 66–67
  non-fiction prose 70–71
  prose fiction 68–69
title 11, 12, 18–19
tone 7, 9, 34
topic 12–13, 18–19

understanding 6
  see also author's attitude; speaker identity; themes

vocabulary see word choice

word choice 7, 9
writing 34–37
  argumentative 56–57
  formal structures 62–65
    rhythm and rhyme 64–65
    stress patterns 63
  free verse and cohesion 66–67
  persuasive 48–49
  reflective 46–47
  style 34–35
  tone 34

Check for misused words

You may already have cut these from your texts, but the following are among some of the most commonly misused words. Check that none still linger.

discreet: careful not to attract notice
discrete: separate and distinct

ensure: to make certain that something will happen
insure: to provide compensation in the event of death, theft, damage etc.

practice: this a noun and should not be confused with ...
practise: the verb

appraise: to assess
apprise: to inform someone of something

affect: to change, influence or to make a difference to something
effect: to bring about a result, to do

climactic: creating, forming a climax
climatic: relating to the climate

complacent: self-satisied, smug, unconcerned
complaisant: willing to please, go along with

disinterested: impartial, with no axe to grind
uninterested: not interested

elicit: to draw out a reaction or a reply
illicit: not permitted by rules or law

imply: to suggest indirectly
infer: to draw a conclusion

Be thoughtful with the thesaurus

A thesaurus puts thousands of words at your disposal. It can enrich your bank of synonyms to an amazing degree. But you have to be careful not to use the first alternative that comes to hand. The possibilities on offer all have slightly different shades of meaning.

Here we have four good synonyms for 'sensitive', but we would use them in very different ways. Always check back with a dictionary for the precise definition of your new synonym before inserting it in your text.

SENSITIVE	thoughtful – She responds well to poetry and is sensitive to what the poet is trying to express.
	thin-skinned – He's sensitive about his height, so be careful what you say.
	tender – My bruises have all healed up but the skin on my arm is still very sensitive.
	top-secret – You need security clearance to be allowed to read information this sensitive.

FINAL EDITING PROCESS
DETAILED CHECKS

Check number agreement

In sophisticated texts of the type you're creating for your dissertation and portfolio, you'll often be dealing with extended, complex sentences. Even experienced writers may at times lose track of the subject's agreement and end up with a plural verb for a singular subject which appeared much earlier in the sentence. Or vice versa.

Avoid vague pronoun referents

Always check that in an extended sentence you make clear what it is that an 'it' or a 'this', or some other pronoun, refers back to. This problem might be most evident at the beginning of a second sentence when the first sentence has had several candidates as possible referents for the 'it' or 'this'. To the writer, the sense is quite clear but, at times, the reader may be left in some confusion.

Avoid sexism

In previous generations, when grammar saw nothing wrong in making the assumption that everyone was male, sentences such as 'Each candidate will be given his exam number by Friday' were common. Now, we can avoid this sexisim by introducing 'Each candidate will be given his/her exam number by Friday.' But the result seems clumsy. Authoritative writing guides now allow us to break what were once cherished rules by saying 'Each candidate will be given their exam number by Friday'. As a solution, it both sounds natural and avoids sexism.

Check citation layout

Tidiness in citation presentation does much to define yourself as a proficient writer. Make sure you offer clarity in differentiating your text from the quoted words. In longer citations, you have choices to make.

Sometimes, you will prepare the reader for the quotation by first describing what it is doing:

> Her clear-sightedness is seen in the words:

We note the description ends in a colon. For the actual citation, we should drop a line and indent the start of the citation so that the complete unit of text becomes:

> Her clear-sightedness is seen in the words:
>
>   'I have betrayed a great man whose like we shall never see again.'

Alternatively, we can simply introduce the citation. In this case, a colon would simply interrupt the natural flow of your comment. So instead, a better presentation is:

> Her clear sightedness is seen when she comments that she has
>
>   'betrayed a great man whose like we shall never see again'.

But here, as above, a line has been dropped and the cited words indented. This allows the citation to stand out from your own text.

Drop another line before continuing with your own text.

contd

SETTING ABOUT REPAIR

Once those localised areas needing attention are identified and rectified, it's a good idea to go over the corrected text once again on your own. Even the best text can be improved.

Take a paragraph at a time

- Check if any claims or statements made in the opening sentence(s) have been supported by adequate evidence.
- Check if you have used the same word too often to launch sentences: 'The', 'It', 'However' and 'Although' are prime candidates here.
- Check also that you have provided sufficient variety of sentence structure and sentence length to prevent the text from beginning to sound turgidly monotonous.

Beware online text checkers

There are a number of websites offering help with grammar, expression, etc. These need to be treated with caution. This writer was able to smuggle two comma-spliced sentences past one, so their usefulness may be severely limited.

Review word choice

In your dissertation, you are writing what should be sophisticated prose analysing complex texts. In your portfolio, you are presenting yourself as a highly proficient wordsmith. In both cases, you can undermine your efforts by casual word choice. Devote a proofreading session to reviewing word choice alone. Check a paragraph at a time to see if your choice of words could be improved in places. In conclusions, where you may be returning to statements you made in your introduction, see if judicial use of synonyms might avoid a sameness of expression creeping in.

Double-check spelling

Yes, that spellchecker on your computer is reliable for tricky words. But, while it's useful for getting 'separate' and 'definitely' correct, has it picked up 'bit' when you meant 'but'? Even with spellcheckers in place, the occasional typo can creep in. Make sure it doesn't. Check paragraph by paragraph as an editing activity on its own.

Scrutinise punctuation

In a creative portfolio piece, is your dialogue punctuation all it should be? In your dissertation, are you making correct use of colons and semi-colons? Are you, indeed, making the most of the usefulness of colons and semi-colons to present information as coherently as possible, in a way that allows your arguments and facts to be easily assimilated? Perish the thought that you might have let a dreaded comma splice slip through. If in doubt at all about the functions of various punctuation marks, see pages 16–19 of the *BrightRed CfE Higher English Study Guide*.

 DON'T FORGET

You've had months to prepare these texts. Imagine what a poor impression you'll make on the examiners if, after all that time, your text still betrays evidence of merely casual editing.